Voices of MILWAUKEE BRONZEVILLE

Voices
—— OF ——
MILWAUKEE BRONZEVILLE

DR. SANDRA E. JONES

Published by The History Press
Charleston, SC
www.historypress.com

Copyright © 2021 by Dr. Sandra E. Jones
All rights reserved

First published 2021

Manufactured in the United States

ISBN 9781467148887

Library of Congress Control Number: 2021941049

Notice: The information in this book is true and complete to the best of our knowledge. It is offered without guarantee on the part of the author or The History Press. The author and The History Press disclaim all liability in connection with the use of this book.

All rights reserved. No part of this book may be reproduced or transmitted in any form whatsoever without prior written permission from the publisher except in the case of brief quotations embodied in critical articles and reviews.

The great migration to Milwaukee stimulated the dream of a Black Metropolis, a city within a city, that would fundamentally cater to the needs of Afro-Americans.

—*Joe William Trotter Jr.*

CONTENTS

Acknowledgements	9
Introduction	11
1. African Americans in Wisconsin	15
Wisconsin's Early Black Settlers	15
Slavery in the Wisconsin Territory	18
Milwaukee's First Black Residents	20
2. Creating Black Boundaries	27
3. Profiles	33
Mamie Thurman	34
Robert "Bobby" Mosley	42
George F. Sanders	48
William "Bill" Nolen Jr.	50
Dr. Reuben Harpole	54
Joseph "Joe" DeCou	56
Raymond Washington	60
Sharon Adams	66
4. Building Community	75
The Neighborhood	75
Community Across Racial, Ethnic and Economic Lines	80

Contents

Work Ethic	82
Lapham Park and the Lapham Social Center	86
Schools	91
Mentoring Children	97
Churches	99
Urban League	102
Regal and Roosevelt Theaters	103
Entertainment	107
5. Leaving Bronzeville	111
New Neighborhoods	115
Notes	119
Bibliography	123
About the Author	125

ACKNOWLEDGEMENTS

I would first like to thank the folks who graciously shared their stories with me and allowed me to share them with the world—Mamie Thurman, Robert Mosley, George F. Sanders, William Nolen, Dr. Reuben Harpole, Joseph DeCou, Raymond Washington and Sharon Adams—and those who read the many drafts of the manuscript and provided valuable feedback: Brenda Coley, Michelle Dodds, Dr. Patrick Bellegarde-Smith, Denise M. Bailey and Stina Baker. And many thanks to John Rodrigue and Ashley Hill, editors at The History Press, for all your support and patience.

INTRODUCTION

Imagine a Milwaukee with horse-drawn wagons traveling down the city street and a man on top yelling, "Oranges, oranges, oranges for sale." When you were a little short of money, you could buy on credit from the corner grocery store to feed your family supper. When milk was left fresh daily in your home's milk box and taverns stayed open all night long. When Lapham Park was the community meeting place, and at some point in the day, everyone stopped there to go swimming, play baseball or take a sewing class. And electric streetcars extended throughout the city. Some people today don't have to imagine—they have only to remember.

This book introduces a few of the men and women who grew up in Milwaukee's oldest African American community, now remembered as Bronzeville. They are the folks who personify *Voices of Milwaukee Bronzeville*:

Mamie (Graham) Thurman
Robert "Bobby" Mosley
George Sanders
William "Bill" Nolen
Dr. Reuben Harpole
Joseph "Joe" DeCou
Raymond Washington
Sharon Adams

Introduction

The published work on Milwaukee's Bronzeville community documents the historical experience of Black Milwaukee.[1] It attempts to reimagine the hustle and bustle of a community of African Americans, a "Black metropolis," a city within a city with thriving businesses and a vibrant social structure. It recounts the tale of a Walnut Street alive, with its many business establishments serving a hardworking, all-Black population determined to make something out of the meager resources available to them. It describes an African American community of yesteryear, complete with strong values and role models for its youth. Religious establishments such as St. Marks Methodist Episcopal, St. Benedict the Moor, Calvary Baptist and St. Matthews CME attended to the spiritual lives of the residents; and the Flame, the Metropole and Satin Doll Nightclubs took care of the entertainment and secular needs of the people. Above all else, these narratives tell the tale of a community united in looking out for the well-being of all within. Adults were responsible for the children, whether that meant expressing loving care or dispensing harsh discipline. Let them tell it—the chastisement you might receive from a neighbor on the street would be nothing compared to what you'd get at home after your misbehavior was reported to your parents.

If the truth is to be told, there is a larger story about the historical experience of Black people in Milwaukee, one that certainly incorporates but goes far beyond the idyllic place called Milwaukee Bronzeville. It is the story of denial and confinement, the story of a subtle yet persistent intercity migration to a leftover and segregated landscape. It is the story of the forced confinement of a people within a designated city area, where the housing stock had long outlasted its livability, a space characterized by overcrowding because it ultimately grew too small to accommodate the expanding African American population. Thus, the historical experience of Black people in Milwaukee has been one of finding ways to maintain a level of dignity and a sense of belonging under the worst of circumstances. For most of its existence, this space that has come to be called Bronzeville was never an all-Black community. Rather, it was the only area in the city where Black people were permitted to live. Initially bordered by Highland Boulevard to the south, Walnut Street to the north, Third Street to the east and Twelfth Street to the west, this space was inhabited by a majority Jewish population. It was not until the 1950s that the area now known as Bronzeville became a majority African American community.

Given its historical experience, rather than a place, Bronzeville can be better reimagined as a spirit, engendered by a people determined to make a way out of no way. That is certainly the overwhelming sense I got as I

Introduction

sat down and talked to the folks who lived that experience. The interview subjects for this book are all African American men and women who were born in Milwaukee and Wauwatosa between the 1920s and the 1940s. They have lived their entire lives, from childhood to adulthood, and tender older years negotiating the trials and the joys of life in Milwaukee. Their families were among the city's earliest Black residents, some having settled in the area as early as 1906. They, indeed, embody the spirit of Milwaukee Bronzeville.

When I started this project, I called it *The Making of Milwaukee Bronzeville*. Rather than center this narrative on the businesses that existed in the area of Walnut Street, which is so often the focus, I wanted to highlight the people who made up Milwaukee's early African American community. What was it like to grow up as a Black person in Milwaukee in the 1920s, 1930s and 1940s? I wanted to explore what life was actually like for the earliest Black Milwaukee residents. My starting place was four men who were born in Milwaukee, who lived and grew up in the Bronzeville area. Bill Nolen, Bobby Mosley, Joe DeCou and Raymond Washington met and became friends when they were young boys playing sports at Lapham Park, and they have remained friends for over sixty years. Today, their families attend the same church on Sundays, and they get together every Friday for swimming and other activities at the Northside YMCA—or they sit around Bill's kitchen table and reminisce. Just to the east lives Mamie Thurman. Ms. Thurman was born in Milwaukee in the 1920s, and her family has lived in the city since 1906. She can often be seen outside her home, tending to her always immaculate yard or hosting large gatherings for her family. Also included are Dr. Reuben Harpole, born in the 1930s and often called the foremost expert on the history of the area, and George Sanders, also born during that time and a journalist and active participant in open housing struggles. Finally included is Sharon Adams, born in the 1940s, who saw, firsthand, the end of the community known as Bronzeville. After being away for many years, Sharon came back to Milwaukee to reclaim her neighborhood.

"Did you all call it Bronzeville when you were growing up?" I asked them. "No" was their unanimous response. "It was just the place where we lived." In fact, an official Bronzeville did exist in Chicago. But the term became a generic label that has historically described areas of cities that housed large African American populations. So, I changed the name of the project to *The Myth of Milwaukee Bronzeville*. However, I quickly realized that the change would offend many who cherish the concept of Milwaukee Bronzeville; it would attempt to erase something that was so real to many African American Milwaukeeans.

Introduction

An interview with Joe DeCou one afternoon sitting in Bill Nolen's kitchen solved the dilemma. He said, "You know, if I could, I would ask God to give me the same life had. I had more good times than bad times." It was then that I realized that Milwaukee Bronzeville was not necessarily a place. It was the spirit of community and comradery that had sustained a friendship for over sixty years. It was the determination that allowed a people to not simply survive but thrive during good times and bad. What's more, their voices and stories have much to teach us today. Thus, the name of the project became and remains *Voices of Milwaukee Bronzeville*.

1

AFRICAN AMERICANS IN WISCONSIN

Wisconsin's Early Black Settlers

African Americans have been a part of Wisconsin's landscape since before the founding of the city of Milwaukee in 1848. A Black presence was recorded in the territory even before Wisconsin became a state. It was those brave pioneers who planted the seeds that would grow into a vibrant Black community in Milwaukee. The Northwest Ordinance of 1787 forbade the existence of slavery in the north lands, including the Wisconsin Territory. And it was initially the pull of freedom that drew Black people to the area. Recorded instances of Black people living in Wisconsin extend back to the 1700s. Historical records indicate that two Black men established a trading post at what is now Marinette, Wisconsin, between 1791 and 1792.[2]

More well known is the story of Jean and Marie Jeanne Bonga, who arrived in the Michigan Territory aboard a British ship in 1782. Both were enslaved by a British officer, Captain Daniel Robertson, during the Revolutionary War. Robertson was the commander of Fort Mackinac in the Michigan Territory.[3] When Robertson died, Jean and Marie Jeanne remained in the area as free persons. The Bongas represent a stable permanence for Wisconsin's Black population. They married and worked in the Michigan and Wisconsin Territories as fur traders. After Jean Bonga died in 1795, his son, Pierre, and grandsons, Stephen and George, continued to live and work in Upper Michigan and Wisconsin as fur traders and interpreters

George Bonga (1802–1874) lived and worked in upper Michigan and Wisconsin as a fur trader and interpreter into the nineteenth century. *Courtesy of the Minnesota Historical Society.*

between the Minnesota and Wisconsin governments and Native tribes into the nineteenth century.[4] George Bonga was the first African American to be born in Minnesota.[5] Stephen Bonga helped organize the Methodist Episcopal Church in Superior, Wisconsin. The Bongas were among the first free African American residents of the state.[6]

Stephen Bonga served as an interpreter in treaty negotiations between the Minnesota government and Ojibwe and Dakota tribes in Wisconsin. In 1850, Bonga and his Ojibwe wife traveled five hundred miles from Wisconsin to Sandy Lake in Minnesota to collect payments promised in the treaty. On their arrival, they discovered that the effort was an attempt to permanently relocate the tribe. The tribe returned to Wisconsin, having lost over four hundred people to hunger over the course of the journey.[7]

There is recorded evidence that other people of African descent resided in the area of Prairie du Chien, Wisconsin, in the 1700s. One of those residents was Marianne La Buche. La Buche was a mixed-race woman of African and French descent who settled in Wisconsin in 1790s. She traveled from the St. Louis area by way of the Mississippi River. From three marriages, she gave birth to thirteen children, who she raised in Prairie du Chien. LaBuche was well known and widely respected for her medical remedies and treatments

ians were frequently joked about Mary Ann's superior skill in the healing art. There are at this time a number of her descendants still residing in Prairie du Chien.—Taken from The Union, February 13, 1902.

The Milwaukee Sunday Journal November 29, 1925.

Woman First State "Doctor"

Settlers Long Healed by Herb Remedies of Aunt Mary Ann

BY SPECIAL CORRESPONDENT OF THE JOURNAL

Prairie du Chien — The first "doctor" to practice in Wisconsin was a woman. She was Mary Ann Labuche, of mixed African and white blood, born at Cahokia, Ill., some time prior to 1774, and came to Prairie du Chien, then Prairie des Chiens, at an early age.

Prior to the coming of the military regime in the middle west, she was a person of consequence among the inhabitants, most of whom knew her as "Aunt Mary Ann." Until a surgeon arrived with the troops, she was called by the sick and attended them as regularly as a physician of the present day.

Dr. William Beaumont, one of the early army surgeons who gained international reputation among scientists while in Prairie du Chien, was the object of many jests in the frontier when Aunt Mary Ann would bring relief with her "yarb tea" to a patient whom he and other physicians had treated and, perhaps for want of good nursing, could not cure.

This first Wisconsin "doctor" was the mother of 14 children. She was three times married. Her first husband was named Duchoquette and one of the two sons born to them died in 1810 on John Jacob Astor's expedition to the Pacific coast to find the mouth of the Columbia in Oregon.

Registe Gagnier, her first son by the second marriage, was killed on June 26, 1827, by Red Bird, an Indian, not far from the spot now occupied by Evergreen cemetery, and his daughter scalped and thrown under the bed of the one room log cabin for dead. Several hours later when neighbors were preparing the 3-year-old child for burial, signs of life were noted and Aunt Mary Ann covered the exposed brain of the infant with a piece of silver, saving its life. The little girl lived 80 years.

A 1925 *Milwaukee Sunday Journal* article on Marianne La Buche, Wisconsin's first female doctor. In 2016, a statue in Mississippi River Sculpture Park was dedicated to La Buche in Prairie du Chien, Wisconsin. *Courtesy of the* Milwaukee Sunday Journal.

that included herbs, midwifery and Native folk medicine. Not much more is known about La Buche. However, a 1925 *Milwaukee Sunday Journal* article identifies her as the first female doctor in the state. A statue in Prairie du Chien's Mississippi River Sculpture Park bears the likeness of Marianne La Buche. Her descendants lived in the area into the twentieth century.[8]

SLAVERY IN THE WISCONSIN TERRITORY

Even though slavery was prohibited in the territory, enslaved Africans lived in many parts of Wisconsin. White settlers who were traveling from southern states to Wisconsin's lead mining region brought enslaved Black people along with them.[9] The 1836 Territorial Census recorded the existence of seventeen enslaved Black people at Fort Crawford in Prairie du Chien.[10] With no formal structures for the existence of slavery, over time, many of these enslaved Black people gained their freedom and remained in the area.[11] Historian John Davidson cites numerous cases of enslaved Black people who acquired their freedom after arriving in Wisconsin with White people in the 1840s. He makes the point that when slavery exists in a community that does not support it as an institution, "we may be sure that it will not last long. So that, as related to the first Negroes brought to Wisconsin, we have a story of liberation rather than one of continuance in bondage."[12] Based on direct witness testimony from people who resided in the area in the 1830s and 1840s, Davidson identifies dozens of instances in which Black people who arrived enslaved gained their freedom in and around Lancaster, Wisconsin, in Grant County. Two Missouri settlers named Ross and Cobb transported between 20 and 30 enslaved Black people to Wisconsin in the 1840s. On gaining their freedom, that group constituted a "colony of coloreds" near Lancaster.[13] Historian John Trotter cites a contingent of free Black people who were reported to have settled near Dodgeville in 1832. The 1840 U.S. census recorded 101 black men and 84 black women in the Wisconsin Territory. By 1850, that number had grown to a total of 655.[14] There is no doubt that some among this number had run away or had entered the state enslaved and gained their freedom after arriving.

The Wisconsin Historical Society's records indicate that Paul Jones actually sued his former owner for back wages once he found himself on Wisconsin's free soil.[15] George Wallach Jones moved to the Wisconsin

Territory in 1831 with his wife and seven enslaved Black people. He later served as surveyor-general of the Wisconsin and Iowa Territories for the Van Buren administration. G.W. Jones allowed Paul, one of the seven enslaved Black people, to work for wages to purchase his freedom. He also released Paul's sister Charlotte and his three nephews from enslavement. Claiming that his enslavement was illegal because Wisconsin was free territory, Paul Jones sued in 1842 to reclaim back wages for his labor and for the price of his purchase.[16] The suit was unsuccessful. Although one of the jurors argued forcefully on Paul's behalf, the other White members of the jury halted the debate and decided that he was not entitled to back wages because they wanted to attend a dog fight that was being held that evening.

The relative safety of Wisconsin's free soil was considerably altered after passage of a strengthened Fugitive Slave Act in 1850. That law gave slaveholders the right to come into free state territories and recapture Black people who had escaped enslavement.[17] Fugitive slave legislation dates back to the Constitutional Convention, when southern slaveholders were successful in including a "Fugitive Slave Clause" in the U.S. Constitution that stipulated

Caroline Quarles; a plaque marking a historic stop on the Underground Railroad tells the story of Caroline Quarles. *Courtesy of the Burlington Historical Society.*

Joshua Glover; a plaque that recounts the story of Joshua Glover's historic rescue and escape to freedom. *Courtesy of the Burlington Historical Society.*

"'no person held to service or labor' would be released from bondage in the event they escaped to a free state." The 1850 legislation revised the previous act by requiring citizens to assist in the capture of said escaped persons. It denied enslaved people the right to a jury trial and imposed a penalty for citizens who interfered or assisted runaways with a $1,000 fine and six months in jail. Many of the Black people who were living in the Wisconsin area had, indeed, escaped enslavement and lived under assumed names. Rather than risk recapture, many fled to Canada.

Another attraction for African American settlers to Wisconsin was the strong antislavery sentiment that grew after the Revolutionary War, when the debate over the issue of slavery raged in the country. Wisconsin became an abolitionist stronghold and a pathway to Canada for Black people escaping to freedom. The two most notable cases of this were those of Caroline Quarlls and Joshua Glover. In 1842, Caroline Quarlls made her way through Milwaukee, escaping enslavement in St. Louis, Missouri. Hers was the first recorded use of the Underground Railroad.[18] Joshua Glover, also escaping enslavement in Missouri, was captured by slave hunters and held in a Milwaukee jail. Abolitionists overran the jailhouse and freed Glover. He was eventually safely transported to Canada.

Milwaukee's First Black Residents

Milwaukee's early Black population can best be characterized as transient. Two factors contributed to this characterization. The first was passage of the 1850 Fugitive Slave Act. The second was economic. Very few opportunities existed for Black people to sustain a livelihood. In the early days Black people were limited to employment as cooks, servants and general laborers.

MILWAUKEE BLACK POPULATION 1840–1990

Year	Black Population	Percentage	Total Population
1990	191,255	30.5	628,088
1980	146,940	30.5	636,212
1970	105,088	23.1	717,099
1960	62,458	8.4	741,324
1950	21,772	3.4	637,392
1940	8,821	1.5	587,472
1930	7,501	1.3	587,249
1920	2,229	.5	457,147
1910	980	.3	373,857
1900	862	.3	285,315
1890	449	.2	204,468
1880	304	.3	115,587
1870	176	.2	71,440
1860	106	.2	45,246
1850	98	.5	20,061
1840	22	1.3	1,712

Nevertheless, the territorial census of 1838 listed fifteen African Americans among Milwaukee's residents. Of that number, eight were men and seven were women.[19] Half of these Black residents lived in homes with White people and were most likely servants. However, there were two independent Black households. One was that of James Foster and his wife, who lived in Milwaukee until they left in 1846.

Joe Oliver was most likely counted in the 1838 territorial census. He was among the city's first Black residents, having traveled to the area in 1835, employed as cook to Solomon Juneau, one of Milwaukee's founders and its first mayor.[20] Oliver actually voted in the first election that was held in the city, becoming the first African American to cast a ballot in Milwaukee. Oliver left the city after two years in 1837 to become a ship's cook on the schooner *Cincinnati* and the *C.C. Trowbridge*. He often retuned to visit Milwaukee before his death in 1842.[21]

In 1840, there were twenty-two Black people among Milwaukee's population. This number constituted the first stable generation of African Americans in the city. William H. Anderson was among that number. Anderson arrived in Milwaukee in 1841. His wife, Ann, the daughter of Sully and Susanna Watson, joined him in 1845.[22] The Andersons set down roots for the oldest continuous Black family in Milwaukee. William Anderson was a staunch abolitionist until his death in 1854. He operated the United States Hotel Barbershop and owned a considerable amount of property in the city.[23] The barber trade appears to have been one that was open to Black people, both in terms of employment and business ownership. William Green headed a household made up of three men and two women. He owned and operated the Emporium of Fashion located on the south side of Wisconsin Street, midway between the alley and East Water Street.[24] Between 1844 and 1845, there were three Black barbers living in Milwaukee: William Morgan, Joseph DeLong and Thomas Brown.

Robert Titball was another notable first-generation Black person to reach Milwaukee. Landing in the city in 1842, Titball and Miss Sarah Abel Brown were among the first African Americans to be married in Milwaukee. Titball opened a barbershop and bathhouse at Sixteenth and Wisconsin Streets and a barbershop at the American House on Third Street. Titball was also known for his role in the Caroline Quarlls incident. Titball spotted Quarlls when she arrived in Milwaukee and suspected that she was a runaway. Initially, he appeared to sympathize with her plight and took her into his household. However, when he learned that there was a $300 reward offered for her capture, Titball reported her whereabouts to authorities. It was only with the help of sympathetic abolitionists that Quarlls was able to avoid capture and eventually escape to Canada. Quarlls lived the rest of her life in Canada, married and gave birth to six children.[25] Titball left Milwaukee in the early 1850s, apparently to avoid a growing number of creditors.[26] Sarah Carroll, an African American woman, bought and redesigned his property on Third Street, opening a popular millinery and dress store in the 1850s.

Throughout the 1840s and 1850s, Milwaukee's Black population continued to grow and stabilize. In 1846, Robert and Hannah Johnson lived on Jackson and Division Streets (now Juneau Avenue), and farmer George Paddock headed a family of six. By 1852, there were forty Black residents listed in the Milwaukee census. Twenty-five (62 percent) lived on the east side, ten (25 percent) lived on the west side and five (13 percent) lived

African Americans in Wisconsin

on the south side. Of the twenty-four children listed, seven were born in Wisconsin. In 1854, five new African American families had relocated to the Milwaukee area. Shoemaker William Henderson, along with his wife and daughter, lived on Third Street, between Spring and Wells Streets. Another Shoemaker, Henry Thompson, lived with his family on Michigan Avenue, between Jefferson and Jackson Streets. Abraham Torrey and his wife took up residence on Fourth Street, between Tamarack and Prairie Streets (now State and McKinley Streets). Ezekiel Gillespie and his family lived at 12 Wisconsin Street. Gillespie would win the right for African Americans to vote in the state in 1866.

By 1880, Milwaukee's African American population numbered 304. It reached 980 by 1910 or about .3 percent of Milwaukee's population. When their numbers were relatively small, African Americans were interspersed with the White population throughout the city. Initially, Black people lived east of the Milwaukee River and in the downtown area; around 1910, a small settlement of Black people lived near Eighth and Tenth Streets, near St. Paul; and about twenty black families resided in Bay View on the south side.[27]

Sully and Susanna Watson, who were among Milwaukee's first African American residents. The Watsons in their home on Mason Street are featured in a 1992 Milwaukee Public Museum installation, the "Streets of Old Milwaukee." *Courtesy of the* Shepard Express.

As the African American population grew, so, too, did their economic stability.²⁸ In the early days, before racial restrictions prohibited Black economic growth, African Americans owned prime property in Milwaukee, especially in the downtown area. Sully and Susanna Watson were one example. When the two met in Richmond, Virginia, Susanna was a free person, and Sully was enslaved on a planation close to where she lived. Sully was allowed to hire himself out as a mason and eventually purchased his own freedom at the price of $500.²⁹ The Watsons relocated to Columbus, Ohio, and lived in that city for sixteen years. When their daughter Ann married a barber named William Anderson and moved to Milwaukee, Sully and Susanna followed in 1850. At the time, there were fewer than one hundred Black people out of a population of twenty thousand living in the city.³⁰ Sully was able to use his masonry skills, and Susanna worked as a seamstress and dressmaker to generate an income. Through their labors, they were able to sustain a comfortable lifestyle. The two accumulated a great deal of wealth and property. They built a home in downtown Milwaukee, where the growing African American community initially settled.

Black people, like the Watsons, uninhibited by restrictions that would later be imposed, were able to purchase land in Milwaukee, and some acquired valuable properties. African Americans owned property on Grand Avenue (Wisconsin Avenue), from Water Street to Broadway Street; on Wells Street, from Fourth to Fifth Streets; and on Wisconsin Avenue, from Second Street to Plankinton Avenue. In 1842, Lyman Benjamin and his wife owned the property where the Plankinton Livery stood on Second Street. They also owned an acre of land in the Ninth Ward. After Benjamin's death in 1883, John Plankinton bought the property where the Plankinton Arcade stands today from real estate dealer John Durbin for $3,375. In 1845, Ambrose Dudley was reported to own property on the block of Fourth and Wells Streets. Jonathan J. Meyer owned a grocery store on Mason Street that was worth $30,000.³¹

As African Americans took up residence in Milwaukee, so began the fight for human and civil rights. Milwaukee's Black history includes many notable events and personalities that shaped important components of the implementation of equal access to civil rights in the city and state. When the 1850 Fugitive Slave Law was enacted, for the first time, African Americans in the city held a community meeting to oppose the measure. Voting rights were also a focus of struggles. Meetings were held and petitions were filed, demanding the right to vote for Wisconsin's Black citizens. In 1857, a petition with three hundred signatures was submitted to the Wisconsin

State Assembly to place a referendum on the next election ballot.[32] While the effort to place the referendum on the ballot was ultimately successful, the measure itself was defeated in the election. It was another ten years before Black suffrage was secured.

The right to vote was finally won by the efforts of another early Black Milwaukee resident. Ezekiel Gillespie came to the city in 1854 with his wife, Sophie, and their three children. He worked as a grocer and eventually became a trusted employee of the Milwaukee Road Company. Gillespie attempted to cast a ballot in the 1865 state election. However, his ballot was rejected by election officials. Gillespie sued the state and won the vote for Black residents in 1866.

Another milestone for African American rights was laid by Attorney William T. Green. He was among the first Black graduates from the University of Wisconsin Law School in 1892, and he was the first Black lawyer in Milwaukee. In 1889, Green helped organize a state convention to demand an end to legal segregation in public places and places of employment. Green and his Union League of Wisconsin successfully filed a lawsuit on behalf of Owen Howell, who was denied a seat on the main floor of the Bijou Opera House in Milwaukee. The suit led to the creation of the Wisconsin Civil Rights Act of 1895, the foundation for the state's modern civil rights legislation. Green was the first Black attorney to argue before the Wisconsin Supreme Court.

Early Black residents also tackled and broke restrictions along the lines of gender. Attorney Mabel Watson Raimey, the granddaughter of Sully and Susanne Watson, was born in Milwaukee in 1895 and was the first African American woman to earn a bachelor's degree from the University of Wisconsin in 1918. She was the first Black woman to enroll in Marquette Law School's evening programs in 1922, and she passed the Wisconsin State Bar in 1927. Ramey opened doors for others, such as Vel Phillips, who became the first Black woman Milwaukee City Council member, the first Black woman to serve as judge and the first Black woman elected Wisconsin's secretary of state.

2

CREATING BLACK BOUNDARIES

As the Black population grew, so, too, did the racial tensions across the city. In the early 1900s, most Milwaukee theaters, hotels and restaurants barred Black customers from their establishments. The change in White attitudes toward African Americans was matched by housing availability. Before 1915, most areas in the city were relatively unrestricted. Early Black settlers in Milwaukee built their homes in and near the downtown area. For example, Sully and Susanna Watson built their home on Mason Street. Robert and Hanna Johnson made their home on Jackson Street. African Americans lived in West Allis and Bay View on Chambers and Hubbard Streets and Oakland, Kinnickinnic and Edison Avenues.[33] In 1901, a group of "high society" Black people who worked as Pullman porters or railway clerks lived between Eighth and Tenth Streets, near St. Paul Avenue.[34] However, over time, things began to change. As racial tensions increased in the city, a slow intercity Black migration began to take place. According to Thomas Buchanan, "By 1908, the great majority of Negroes lived on the west side in a fifteen-block square bounded by Wisconsin on the south, State Street on the north, Third on the east, and Eighth on the west."[35] Buchanan's work includes a series of maps that diagram the gradual movement of Black residents from different areas of the city to a concentrated and segregated area west of the Milwaukee River and north of downtown. Between 1852 and 1915, that gradual movement was nearly complete. By the 1920s, the boundaries of Black Milwaukee began to solidify.

Beyond the growing racial tensions, two other factors continued to drive the Black population to the north and west. The first was demographics. The influx of newly arriving Italian immigrants from Europe forced Black residents away from the east side. Starting in the 1890s, growing numbers of Italian immigrants came to Milwaukee, settling around the edges of downtown and the Third Ward area between the Milwaukee River and Lake Michigan. The Italian population grew from a few hundred in 1880 to 1,740 in 1900 and 4,788 in 1910.[36] Newly arriving Italian immigrants did not only compete with African Americans for low-wage jobs; their growing population also competed for low-cost housing. Black residents were pushed farther west, into the Jewish neighborhoods across the river.

Originally, the Bronzeville area was the home to Milwaukee's Jewish population that had immigrated from Germany, Russia, Ukraine, Lithuania and Poland starting in the mid-1800s. By 1910, the Jewish population numbered ten thousand, initially located north of the downtown and the lower east side areas. The Jewish community was bordered by Third Street to the east and Thirteenth Street to the south; Juneau Avenue to the south and North Avenue to the north.[37] This was the same residential migration pattern that Black residents would follow in later years. The Jewish population expanded to the Sherman Park neighborhoods to the north and west. However, increasing segregation restrictions and restrictive covenants prevented Black people from expanding into these areas.

By the 1940s, the boundaries of the black community, what would come to be considered Bronzeville, were Highland Avenue to the south, Walnut Street to the north, Twelfth Street to the west and Third Street to the east. Even at this time, Black people were still a minority of the population in this area.[38] Black residents would initially share this space with Jewish and German populations. For decades to come, housing segregation meant that this was the only area in which Black people were permitted to live.

The second factor that drove the migration patterns of Black residents was development of the downtown area. Commercial and light industrial plants pushed Black residents out of the areas around Wisconsin Avenue and State Street. As the population of Milwaukee grew, attention to city planning, including land use and management, became more and more of a priority. Changes in municipal zoning of industrial areas expanded the development of the central business district (CBD) and encroached on much of the residential housing on the northern edges of downtown, including on State Street. Early city planning embraced the "City Beautiful" Movement that featured spacious neoclassical architectural designs, with wider streets and pedestrian walk ways.[39] Specifically, the civic center construction and redesign—the auditorium (1909), Milwaukee County Courthouse (1932), the Milwaukee Arena (1950) and the state office building (1963)—required vastly more space and pushed the residential area where Black residents lived to the north. Subsequent civic center construction effectively created the southern border for Bronzeville.

A third factor blocked further movement of the Black population to the west and north of Walnut Street. Restrictive covenants in White neighborhoods that grew in popularity in the 1920s prohibited African Americans from "purchasing, owning, leasing or occupying" housing in "White areas." The refusal of financial institutions to approve mortgage loans for African Americans further limited the ability of Black people to acquire housing in neighborhoods such as Sherman Park and other parts of the city.

Redlining and restrictive covenants limited the ability of African Americans to purchase or build homes in the city. Redlining policies from banks operated in the following way:

> *Some banks marked a red line on a map to indicate an area where they would not loan money. Those areas were most often African American inner city neighborhoods. Because of redlining, many African Americans could not get the loans they needed to buy homes. In addition, some Milwaukee citizens refused to sell their homes to African Americans and moved out of the city as more African Americans moved in. This "White flight" created a very segregated Milwaukee that still exists today.*[40]

As a result of these policies, it was virtually impossible for Black people to buy houses. In 1930, only ten homes were owned by Black people in Milwaukee. The overwhelming majority of Black families rented largely run-down housing in overcrowded areas.[41]

Restrictive covenants were formal and informal agreements among White people to prevent Black people from buying or renting homes in White neighborhoods. These agreements existed in 90 percent of county deeds filed between 1910 and 1940.[42] Signage indicating restrictive housing hung in neighborhoods and suburbs from the 1920s to the 1950s. One sign at the Wauwatosa city limits read: "Entering Wauwatosa City of Homes Restrictive Zoning."[43]

Over time, the boundaries of the Black community had been established. They were confined to where the housing stock was already deteriorated. A 1946 housing study found that 67 percent of African Americans lived in homes that were "unfit for use" or "in need of major repair."[44] The African American population numbered 2,229 or .5 percent of a total Milwaukee population of 457,147. By 1930, the Black population totaled 7,501 or 1.3 percent of 587,249. By 1940, Black people numbered 8,821 or 1.5 percent of the total Milwaukee population of 587,472. As the African American population continued to expand, the choices available to them were still extremely limited. Out of necessity, the increased population pushed the boundaries of the "inner core," and by the 1960s, the community reached Keefe Avenue to the north, Juneau Avenue to the south, the Milwaukee River to the east and Twenty-First Street to the west.

With the broader community largely closed to them, Black people did what Black people do: they made a way out of no way. They built their own. When they could not secure employment elsewhere, they hired their own. According to Ivory Abena Black, 40 percent of the people who lived in Bronzeville worked in Bronzeville. An article by Tula Connell states:

> *The number of self-employed African Americans reached its peak in the 1950s, with Black-owned restaurants, shops, and hotels filling the nine-block stretch of Walnut Street, Bronzeville's Main Street (Vick 1993). From 1940 to 1950, black-owned businesses nearly doubled, growing from 109 to 210. The 1950–1951 Negro Business Directory of the State of Wisconsin listed more than 150 licensed rooming houses, thirty-five taverns, dozens of restaurants and eating establishments, twenty-one dry cleaners, fourteen beauty shops, nine barbershops, and eleven grocery stores, along with eight attorneys, seven doctors, six dentists, eleven entertainers, and nine orchestras.*[45]

If we mark its beginning in the 1920s, Bronzeville proper existed for a relatively short time span, just forty short years. Of course, we know that the destruction of that community was assured when the city adopted policies of urban renewal and constructed the Marquette Interchange and Highway I-43. Between 1960 and 1968, the city demolished 8,500 houses in the central city to facilitate urban renewal projects, and highway construction began in 1964. That highway project went right through the heart of the Black community.

This is the legacy out of which my interview subjects grew. Their families were among the first generation of Black Milwaukeeans who resided in what can properly be called Bronzeville. Alternatively known as the "Inner Core," "Sixth Ward" and "Little Africa," Bronzeville grew out of a spirit—a spirit of determination to make a way out of no way. It emerged from the families who traveled to Milwaukee from distant places to build better lives for their children. It came from Joe Oliver, the Black Milwaukee pioneer who became one of the city's founding residents and the first African American to cast a vote in a city election. It grew from Sully and Susanna Watson, a first family who acquired substantial means in the city. It emerged from the parents of the Thurmans and Mosleys, who ventured north from distant lands in the 1920s to build the first critical mass of Black folk in the city. It sprang from the Nolens, Harpoles, Washingtons, DeCous and the Fosters, whose children would live and play and grow on Walnut, Vine and Somers Streets. These people are among the pioneers who created the community and the spirit of Milwaukee Bronzeville.

3

PROFILES

The *Wisconsin Enterprise Blade*, an early African American newspaper, issued a call: "Let the exodus continue. Let them come, and let their brethren and kindred welcome them, and see that they are not exploited while becoming accustomed to their surroundings."[46] Many heeded the newspaper's call. The number of Black residents in Milwaukee increased from 2,229 in 1920 to 8,821 in 1940. Existing Black families were joined by other family members and friends who were also looking for better jobs and better lives in Milwaukee. The neighborhood expanded northward, past Walnut Street to North Avenue, and westward to Seventeenth Street. While White people continued to make up 50 percent of the population, the area became known as the "Negro district." Because their numbers were still relatively small, many in the Black community knew each other. The African American population included people with varied backgrounds and different class positions. This is the era and neighborhood that the subjects interviewed for this project remember, when the solid boundaries of Black Milwaukee were well established. These folks lived within blocks of each other. They went to the same schools and churches. They shopped in the same stores. They played in the same parks. What follows are their stories, recounting their experiences in their own voices.

Mamie Thurman

Mamie Thurman was born in Wauwatosa, Wisconsin, in 1927 at the Milwaukee County Hospital. Ms. Thurman's family was in the third generation of continuous Black families in Milwaukee. Her father, Emmett Graham, came to Milwaukee from Topeka, Kansas, in 1906. Her mother, Inez Culp, arrived in the city from Chicago in 1910. At the time, there were fewer than one thousand African Americans in the city, making them among the earliest Black families in the city. Eventually, other relatives joined the family in Milwaukee, including Mamie's maternal grandmother, Mamie (Culp) Anderson; two aunts, Myrtle Johnson and Ruth Noland; and cousins Wesley Culp, Georgette Weaver, Ruth First and Lola Winston.

Like many early African American Milwaukee residents, the family converted to Catholicism and were members of St. Benedict the Moor Catholic Church. The Milwaukee Archdiocese began its ministry to African Americans in Milwaukee in 1908. After gaining the church's sanction, African American layman Captain Lincoln Valle and his wife, Julia Yoular, started a small storefront church at 274 Fourth Street. One year later, the church moved to 530 State Street and was formally named St. Benedict the Moor. Its final location was 1041 North Ninth Street, an area with a significant African American population.[47] Mamie remembers that the church and school were just across the street from where her family

Mamie Thurman today, sitting in her home on East Garfield Avenue in Brewers Hill. *Courtesy of Sandra Jones.*

Profiles

Above: Mamie Thurman with a picture of some of her great-grandchildren. *Courtesy of Sandra Jones.*

Left: At the age of ninety-four, Mamie Thurman is often seen working in her yard. *Courtesy of Sandra Jones.*

Left: Mamie's mother Inez Graham pictured with grandchildren. *Courtesy of Mamie Thurman.*

Right: A 1916 letter from Emmet to Inze. Emmett was in Kansas, attending to family business, when he sent this letter to Inez in Milwaukee. *Courtesy of Mamie Thurman.*

lived. St. Benedict soon opened an elementary school and then a high school, and that is where the Graham children received their educations. Emmett and Inez were married at the church, and it is where Mamie and her siblings were baptized. Her father was a very active member of the St. Benedict congregation and served as president of St. Benedict's Holy Name Society.

When Mamie was born, the fifth of the Thurmans' eight children, the family lived in a duplex at 717 West State Street, just across from where the Safety Building is currently located. They moved from State Street to 1030 West Somer Street. Later, they moved to 2119 North Fifth Street and lived there for seventeen years. Because the Black community was small and

Profiles

 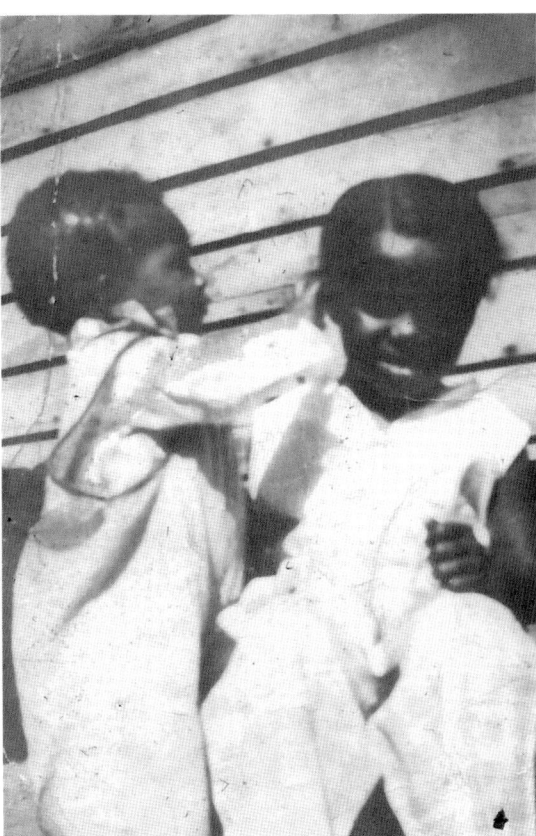

Left: Mamie Anderson at the age of ninety. The grandmother of Mamie Thurman was being honored as the oldest woman in the Happy Days Club. *Courtesy of Mamie Thurman.*

Right: Young Mamie Thurman (*right*). *Courtesy of Mamie Thurman.*

contained in a segregated section of the city, Mamie's family lived in close quarters with some well-known Milwaukee residents. Isaac Coggs was the first African American elected to the Wisconsin state legislature. Also in the neighborhood was Attorney James Dorsey, who has been referred to as the "mayor of Bronzeville" and who ran for alderman 1936 in Milwaukee's Sixth Ward. Le Roy J. Simmons, a member of the Wisconsin State Assembly from 1945 to 1952, also lived there. Mamie remembers, "I did a lot of walking and signing up people to vote."

Emmett Graham worked at a nightclub and gambling establishment called the Metropole Club, located on Fourth Street and Highland Boulevard, one of the neighborhood's most popular night spots. He eventually gained

(From right to left) Mamie and her sisters Dorothy, Patricia and Joyce. *Courtesy of Mamie Thurman.*

Mamie's brothers *(from left to right)*: Wesley, Emmitt Jr., Eugene and Robert. *Courtesy of Mamie Thurman.*

Profiles

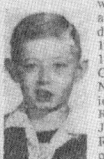

Above: A newspaper notice of Emmet Graham's death. *Courtesy of the* Milwaukee Journal.

Left: Mamie's sister Frances receives her bachelor's degree. *Courtesy of Mamie Thurman.*

Left: Mamie and her husband, Raymond Thurman. *Courtesy of Mamie Thurman.*

Below: Mamie and Raymond Thurman. *Courtesy of Mamie Thurman.*

Opposite: Gayle, Mamie's daughter, reading with a young friend. *Courtesy of Mamie Thurman.*

Profiles

employment as a janitor and motor tester at the International Harvester Company. Sometime in the early 1950s, Mamie's father took a gun from a man who had shot someone on Seventh Street, between Walnut and Vine Streets. He tackled the man, and in the process, he broke his leg. He was able to hold the man until the police arrived at the scene. After the event, Emmett was written up in the *Milwaukee Journal* and called a hero for his bravery. In 1962, at the age of sixty-six, Emmett died after he was hit by a car while crossing the street on Seventh and Galena Streets.

Mamie's mother worked as a cook for a short time at St. Hedwig's Church on Humboldt and Brady Streets, and she also worked cleaning houses. However, with nine children to raise, she was primarily a stay-at-home mom.

Mamie and her sibling attended St. Benedict's School located at 1041 North Ninth Street. She transferred to St. Francis and stayed there through the eighth grade. She returned to St. Benedict for three years. She finished her twelfth-grade year and graduated from Lincoln High School.

Mamie was three years old when she first met her future husband, Raymond Thurman. He was thirteen years her senior. Raymond was a roomer in the boardinghouse run by Mamie's aunt. They were married on

April 5, 1947. Throughout their entire marriage, Raymond was employed as a tannery worker at Pfister and Vogel and the Cudahy Tanning Company. They raised five children: Eugene, Gail, Bradley, Raven and Monique. While Mamie was primarily a stay-at-home mom, she did some work at Krasno Brothers Glove Company, Rabinovitch Millinery Shop and the post office. She also did janitorial work at Brown Street, Garden Homes and Cass Street School.

While homeownership was limited for African Americans, some Bronzeville residents did own property. Mamie's grandmother Mamie Anderson and aunt Ruth Noland owned a home together at 729A West Vliet Street, between Vliet and McKinley Streets. They left the house when the city started constructing the Hillside Projects. Eventually, when Mamie and her husband, Raymond Thurman, purchased a home on East Garfield Avenue in Brewer's Hill, her grandmother moved in with the family. Mamie's grandmother lived to be ninety-seven years old.

Robert "Bobby" Mosley

Robert "Bobby" Mosley was born at County Hospital in 1938 to Waymond and Julia Mosley. His maternal grandparents, Jesse and Viola Tucker, arrived in Milwaukee in 1917 from Cedar Rapids, Iowa, when his mother was one year old. They were originally from Louisiana, Missouri. Bobby's grandfather received training at the Tuskegee Institute and was a master machinist. Milwaukee was known as the machine capital of the world, and Jesse was able to find employment. The Tuckers initially lived on at 814 West Eighth Street. However, because Jesse worked on the south side, the family relocated to that side of town for a time. The Tuckers were among a group of twenty Black families who lived in Bay View in the 1920s.

Bobby's paternal grandparents, James and Jeanette Mosley, arrived in Milwaukee in 1919, also from Cedar Rapids, Iowa. They originated from Atchison, Kansas. They lived in tenement housing on State Street, near St. Benedict the Moor Church. The Mosley children received their elementary education in Catholic school, attending St. John's Lutheran School.

Growing up, Waymond and Julia lived across the street from each other. They were both students at Lincoln High School. Bobby said his father was one of only three Black students in his class back in the 1920s. Waymond was employed as a maintenance man for the Great Lakes Malleable

Profiles

Above: Robert "Bobby" Mosley. *Courtesy of Sandra Jones.*

Right: Bobby (ten, *first row, center*) with his mother, Julia; aunt; and sisters, Mildred (eleven) and Beverly (nine). *Courtesy of Robert Mosley.*

Profiles

Opposite, top: Bobby (*second row, right*) pictured with his classmates at St. Benedict. *Courtesy of Robert Mosley.*

Opposite, middle: Julia Tucker (*last row, third from left*), Bobby's mother, and uncle William "Gus" Tucker (*second row, third from right*) at St. John's Lutheran School in 1920. *Courtesy of Robert Mosley.*

Opposite, bottom: Julia Tucker (*third row, third from right*), Bobby's mother, and uncle William "Gus" Tucker (*fourth row, center*) at St. John's Lutheran School in 1922. *Courtesy of Robert Mosley.*

This page: Bobby's father, Waymond Mosley, in his senior picture at Lincoln High School (*fourth row, second from right*) in 1927. *Courtesy of Robert Mosley.*

Waymond Mosley was one of the three Black students and the only Black male student in his high school class at Lincoln High School in 1926. *Courtesy of Robert Mosley.*

Company and worked as a maintenance man for a number of businesses in what is now the Grand Avenue Mall. He later became a barber. In 1941, when the A.O. Smith Company became a defense plant and started hiring African Americans in significant numbers, Bobby's father found work there. He stayed at A.O. Smith for twelve years and later found employment at the American Motors Company. When Bobby was born,

Profiles

Bobby Mosley (*last row, farthest to the left*) on the St. Benedict basketball team. *Courtesy of Robert Mosley.*

one of seven children, the family lived on Seventh and Reservoir Streets. Shortly afterward, they moved to a home around the corner on Walnut Street, where Bobby spent his first fifteen years.

The second-generation Mosley children continued their family's education tradition by attending Catholic school. Bobby went to St. Benedict the Moor from elementary to high school. He was an exceptional student, carrying a 4.0 grade point average. He was active in extracurricular activities and was a member of St. Benedict's basketball team.

Bobby started working at the age of fourteen, "I always had some kind of job. In high school I worked....I worked at the American Motors. I worked at General Merchandise." He alternated working with attending college. "After high school, I went to Marquette. That was back in the day when you didn't have to take student loans. I started Marquette as a ward of the city." Bobby also holds the distinction of being the first boy to receive a scholarship from Alpha Kappa Alpha (AKA) Sorority: "They listed in the [*Milwaukee*] *Journal*, 'The first boy, Robert Mosley, 718 West Walnut, to receive a $150 scholarship from the AKA Sorority.' And what people don't realize—you know what tuition was back in the day? $450! And then I got a $300 scholarship from Marquette to make up the whole $450."

Bobby was drafted into the army in 1958, and he served for two years. He was initially stationed at Fort Leonard Wood in Missouri and then in Fort Knox in Kentucky. He was then deployed to Germany for thirteen months. After being discharged in 1960, he worked at Inland Steel and A.O. Smith. At the same time, he continued his studies at Marquette, and he graduated in 1965. Bobby ultimately built a thirty-five-year career, working in finance and banking, and was a loan officer at First Wisconsin National Bank. He also worked at North Milwaukee State Bank, the first Black bank in the city, located on Twentieth Street and North Avenue.

Bobby married Linnie Andrews, who came to Milwaukee from Mississippi. They met through a mutual school friend whose wife was a cousin of Linnie's. Linnie was active in the civil rights movement and marched for open housing with Father James Groppi. When the two decided to tie the knot, Father Groppi performed the ceremony at St. Boniface Church. Robert remembers, "And he married us in August of 1967. In fact, we got married right after the riots. When we had our reception, the curfew was going on, and everything had to be done by nine o'clock that day. Everybody had to leave." The couple had two children, Denise and Kurt. Linnie attended vocational school for clerical work. She also worked as a nurse's aide at the VA hospital and as an office manager for the Legal Aid Society.

GEORGE F. SANDERS

George Sanders was born in Milwaukee in 1931. I asked George which hospital he was born in, and he replied, "Hospital? What hospital? I was born in a cold-water flat on Third and Walnut Street."

Both of George's parents were originally from Tennessee. George says that his father, Henderson Sanders, was one of those Black men who couldn't stay in the South. "He didn't want to. My dad traveled around quite a bit, which was sometimes the only option that a lot of Black males had during that time if you had an attitude. Black males had to be careful."

George's parents arrived separately in Milwaukee in the late 1920s. Mattie George, his mother, originated from Gallatin, Tennessee, and was the first of his family to arrive in the city. Mattie had a sister who later joined her in Milwaukee. According to George, both of his parents came north to Milwaukee because life was much better there than it was in the South. Henderson worked a variety of jobs, including one at Allis Chalmers and the Milwaukee Northshore Railroad, where George got his first job at the age of sixteen.

For many years, George's family lived in a cold-water flat at 2136B North Sixth Street, between Lloyd Street and Garfield Avenue. When he was in junior high school, the family moved a block away to Sixth Street and North Avenue, where they lived over a tavern. He remembers it as an integrated neighborhood with poor people everywhere. However, he also remembers that there were some people who enjoyed the higher income, "I know that people across the street and people next door were not so poor. There was an amalgamation of both rich people and poor people living in the same neighborhood. And, of course, that changed when a certain group of people began to do blockbusting."

George was the oldest of three children. He, his brother Henderson Jr. and his sister Barbara, went to public schools. George attended Ninth Street School for elementary and Roosevelt for junior high school. Like most African American children in the city at that time, George attended Lincoln High School and graduated in 1949.

George met Beverly Butka when he was still in high school. "She was one of a group of middle-class White girls attracted to the hipness of Walnut Street, especially the music. The White girls flooded the inner city, particularly Walnut Street. Because we had the dance thing, we had the music and everything. All of a sudden, there were young White girls all over the place." Teenagers hung out at Walnut Street establishments, such as T Joe's Restaurant and Larry's Ice Cream Parlor.

Before leaving for the service, in 1951, George and Beverly married. "I got married when I was getting ready to take a plane to go overseas. I think it was 1951. We took off. Nobody knew anything. We took off, went down to Chicago, my wife and I. We snuck off and got married. Well, you know, you feel I'm going over there and she's here. But you come back." When he returned from the army, he and Beverly lived with his parents in the old neighborhood. They raised four children: two girls, Jill and Kim, and two boys, Brian and Scott.

George was in the army between 1951 and 1953 and served in the Korean War. Afterward, he entered a two-year graphic design course and graduated from Milwaukee Area Technical College. George held many jobs over the years. He worked as a graphics manager for the *Milwaukee Star*, a Black community newspaper founded in 1961. He sold insurance for the Mammoth Insurance Company. For three years, George worked at American Motors Corporation on the Rambler construction line. For nine years, he worked in the Department of Local Affairs in the administration of Governor Warren P. Knowles. His job was to help improve the government's relationship with Black citizens. George was also instrumental in the school desegregation struggles in the 1960s. As one of the "Freedom Walkers for Milwaukee," he taught Black history lessons in the Freedom Schools that were set up for children taking part in the boycott of Milwaukee Public Schools.

WILLIAM "BILL" NOLEN JR.

William "Bill" Nolen, Jr. was born on August 9, 1939, in Milwaukee, Wisconsin, at St. Anthony's Hospital. When he was one year old, his family moved to 1806 North Ninth Street, where they lived until Bill was about fourteen years old. The family then moved one block away, to Tenth and Vine Streets, across the street from the Milwaukee Urban League.

Bill's parents, William Sr. and Vivian (George) Nolen, and older sister Marion, moved to Milwaukee from Sioux City, Iowa, in 1923. His father, a trained butcher, worked in a meatpacking plant in Iowa. When he was able to secure employment at Patrick Cudahy in Milwaukee, the family decided to make the move. Many Black people in Milwaukee were born in Waukesha at the Milwaukee County Hospital. But because his father had health insurance through his employment, Bill was born at St. Anthony's Hospital in Milwaukee.

Bill's mother was a homemaker for most of his childhood. She eventually worked at Vogue Cleaner's on Fourth and Vine Streets. She was excellent at crocheting and would share her skills with her neighbors. In fact, that is how she learned to speak Yiddish. She and one of her Jewish neighbors would sit at her kitchen table for hours. She taught her friend to crochet, and her friend taught her to speak Yiddish.

Bill Attended Ninth Street Elementary School and graduated from the sixth grade at Lee Street School. He went to Roosevelt Junior High School and finally graduated from North Division High School in 1958. It was at that time that his family moved into the newly constructed additions of the Hillside Terrace Housing Projects.

Profiles

Right: Bill Nolen holding a portrait of his grandson Josh. *Courtesy of Sandra Jones.*

Below: Annie and Bill Nolen. *Courtesy of William Nolen.*

Above, left: A portrait of Annie Nolen, Bill's wife. *Courtesy of Sandra Jones.*

Above, right: *Nursing Mother*, by Bill Nolen. *Courtesy of Sandra Jones.*

Left: *Jazz Musician*, by Bill Nolen. *Courtesy of Sandra Jones.*

Profiles

After high school, Bill followed his passion and attended Layton School of the Arts for two years. His interest in art developed when he was a young boy in grade school. He started out doing figure and anatomy drawing. "I did flowers for my mom. She had a picture of some poppies that I did for her that hung in her house for forty years." A teacher at Roosevelt encouraged Bill to pursue his talent, telling him that he had an artistic eye. And he remembers going to O'Bee Funeral Home at 615 West Walnut Street to look at the extensive collection of Black art that hung on their walls. When Bill was fourteen years old, he met well-known Wisconsin artist Karl Priebe at his uncle's tavern: "I used to work in there before school, stacking beer bottles and sweeping the floors." But it was at Layton that he started painting.

Bill was able to employ his artistic skills, designing window displays at Gimble Schuster's on Third Street until he was drafted into the army. He started his service at the beginning of the Vietnam War, although he never served overseas. He received training in dentistry in the army and used that training to secure employment at Mosley Otto Dental Lab on Sixteenth Street and Wisconsin Avenue, making dental implants after he was discharged. He left after six months to start his employment at the Veteran Administration's dental lab, where he stayed for thirty-one years.

The Nolen family attended St. Mark Methodist Episcopal Church, where Bill was baptized. He later converted to Catholicism.

Bill met Annie Thomas, the woman he would marry and share his life with, in 1965, when they both lived in apartment at the Hillside Housing Projects. Annie had traveled from Baton Rouge, Louisiana, to Chicago, Illinios, looking for job opportunities. She arrived in Milwaukee in 1963, while Bill still served in the army. They met one day as Annie was having a new television set delivered to her apartment. Bill offered to help the delivery man bring the set up the stairs to her apartment. Annie said that the two didn't start dating right away, but "he just wouldn't stop coming around." They dated for ten years before finally tying the knot in 1975. Annie worked at Inryco Steel Inc. for nineteen years as an office clerk in the accounting department. She also worked at the Blackhawk Leather Company and Sid Grinker Fire Restoration Company on Fourth and Walnut Street. Together, Bill and Annie raised four daughters, Bridget, Sherly, Cynthia and Marva.

Dr. Reuben Harpole

Dr. Reuben Harpole was born at Milwaukee County Hospital in Wauwatosa, Wisconsin, on September 4, 1934. At the time, his family lived on Fourth Street and Garfield Avenue in a red-brick house. Reuben's mother, Mardee Johnson, and maternal grandparents, James Wesley and Geneva Johnson, arrived in Milwaukee from Little Rock, Arkansas. James had secured a job at Wisconsin Grey Iron Foundry as a crane operator. His father, Reuben K. Harpole, came from Kansas City to finish his high schooling so that he could attend college. His parents met as students at Lincoln High School. When Reuben was eight years old, his parents separated, and his father moved to Detroit, Michigan. He, his two sisters Marjorie and Gloria, and his mother moved in with his grandparents at 807 West Somers Street. That is where Reuben grew up. Mardee was a dental assistant and also worked for a time at the Milwaukee County Hospital. When Reuben's grandfather bought a store across the street from their home, Mardee also worked there for a time. After a while, Reuben's mother left the family and went back south. He and his sisters, Gloria and Marjorie, were then raised by his grandparents. Reuben's family left Sommers Street when the freeway construction began.

Reuben Harpole. *Courtesy of Sandra Jones.*

Reuben's grandfather James, played a significant role in his upbringing and was a great influence in his life. In addition to working at Grey Iron Foundry, he opened a grocery store on Somers Street, sold coal to the neighborhood families to heat their homes and operated a rental bicycle station. According to Reuben:

> *My grandfather's bicycles would be twenty-five cents an hour and fifty cents for three hours. And every time they'd have a parade downtown, my grandfather would decorate the wheels different colors, and then he gave the young people who rode in the parade a white sailor's cap. And then it'd be about thirty bicycles and people parading behind the parade downtown.*

Reuben attended Ninth Street Elementary School, Roosevelt Junior High School and North Division High School. He graduated from North Division in 1953. His sisters attended school at St. Benedict.

The family attended Mount Calvary Holy Church, where Reuben was greatly influenced by many great preachers.

Reuben met his life partner, Mildred (Cowan) Harpole, when she was a student at Marquette University in Milwaukee. When Reuben and Mildred first met, he thought he was not articulate enough to keep up with her. He tried to introduce her to another friend from his church: "Julius. His name was Julius Caesar. He was the brother of the famous gospel singer Shirley Caesar." But Mildred, apparently, had her sights set on Reuben. He started escorting her to dances and taking her to dinner. In 1953, Reuben was drafted into the army. However, he never told Mildred when he was leaving for basic training. He was sent to San Antonio, Texas. Mildred left Marquette to attend law school at Howard University in Washington, D.C. Then, one day, he received a phone call.

> *I'm at Fort Sam Houston in Texas. I thought I had gotten away. I hear an announcement on the loudspeaker: "Phone call for Reuben Harpole." I said, "What?" I cross the street, picked up the phone. And I said, "Hello." I kept thinking to myself, who knows I'm down here? And she said, "So, what are you gonna do?" I proposed to her then, it was the 14 of February."*

Reuben served his time in the Korean War, and Mildred completed her law studies. The couple was married on August 29, 1959. Both were heavily involved in community service and politics over the years. They raised three children: Pasty, Annette and John.

The Harpoles have often been thought of as a "quintessential power couple" in the Milwaukee community. Both have made significant contributions in the area of education, housing and civil rights. Reuben entered the University of Wisconsin–Milwaukee (UWM) and earned a bachelor's degree in elementary education in 1978. He eventually worked for the UWM School of Continuing Education for thirty-one years as a senior outreach specialist at the University Center for Urban Community Development. In 1998, he went to work as a program officer for the Helen Bader Foundation (now Bader Philanthropies Inc.), where he spearheaded the selection of 758 grants, totaling more than $6.4 million. He was awarded an honorary doctorate degree of human letters from UWM in 2005. Reuben is well known as the "Black mayor of Milwaukee," possessing the institutional memory of the history of Bronzeville. Mildred Harpole was an advocate for education equality. She was a founder of the 1964–65 Freedom Schools, advocating for African American history during the school integration struggles. She also became a reading specialist in Milwaukee Public Schools. With the U.S. Department of Housing and Urban Development, Mildred fought to create equal housing in the city.

JOSEPH "JOE" DECOU

If I had to go back again, I'd tell God to raise me the same way. I had more good times than bad times. I had breakfast, lunch and supper.
—*Joe DeCou*

Joe DeCou was born, officially, in Wauwatosa, Wisconsin, at Milwaukee County Hospital in 1939. But according to his mother, he was born on Eleventh and Walnut Streets when she was on her way to the hospital. Assuming the voice of his mother, he says, "You wasn't born in no Wauwatosa. You came out of me when they was taking me down the steps on Eleventh and Walnut. You was raising all kinds of hell. You was hollering more than I was hollering."

Joe's father, Edward Placide DeCou, left New Orleans with his brother in search of better jobs. Their first stop was Chicago. Having no luck finding work in that city, they headed the ninety miles north to Milwaukee in 1937. Joe's father was able to secure employment at Plankinton Packing House. Plankinton Packing began hiring Black workers during World War I. It was only after he had employment and a furnished home for the family that Joe's mother, Maude, joined him. According to Joe, "She told my daddy, 'I'm not coming up there until you find the house, and pay the rent, and get some furniture.'" That first home was located on Eleventh and Walnut Streets.

Edward and Maude had six children. Joe's oldest sister, Joyce, was born in New Orleans. He and his other siblings, Marvin, Roy, Beverly and Vera, were born in Milwaukee. As the family grew, they moved two blocks away to 917A West Walnut Street, the heart of the Black community's business district. Joe recalls, "That was the heart of the core. Ninth and Walnut, that was the middle of all the businesses. It went from Twelfth and Walnut all the way down to Third and Walnut." The children attended St. Benedict the Moor School on Tenth and State Streets from first to twelfth grade.

Profiles

Top: Joe DeCou. *Courtesy of Joe DeCou.*

Bottom: The DeCou family. (*Front row, left to right*): Beverly, Vera, Maude (mother) and Joyce. (*Back row, left to right*): Roy, Joe and Marvin. *Courtesy of Joe DeCou.*

Voices of Milwaukee Bronzeville

Marvin Decou

Left: Marvin DeCou, Joe's brother. *Courtesy of Joe DeCou.*

Below: Joe DeCou (*right*) with his brother Roy and friend Kenneth Townsend. *Courtesy of Joe DeCou.*

Opposite: Joe DeCou's singing group, the Keynotes, performing at the Milwaukee Arena. (*From left to right*): John Wilder, Gerald "PeeWee" Lawrence, Bill Hegwood and Joe DeCou. *Courtesy of Joe DeCou.*

Roy Decou   Kenneth Townsend   Joe Decou

Joe's father eventually found work at Allis Chalmers. After a time, his parents separated, and the family lived on welfare. His mother also did day work, cleaning houses for White families to support her family.

Joe started working, even before high school, in about six or seventh grade. He got a paper route, sold bottles and rags, whatever he could find to make money. When Joe was nine years old, he had a shoe shine box that he used to shine shoes. A carpenter friend made it for him, and he scratched "fifteen cents," the cost of a shoe shine, on the side of the box with a nail. Joe took his box down to the Milwaukee Railroad. Black sailors and soldiers coming from Chicago to Milwaukee would get off the trains. When they ran across a youngster trying to make some money, they would try to help him out by getting their shoes shined. He still has that box today.

While in high school at St. Benedict, Joe's passion was singing. Along with two ninth-grade friends—John Wilder and Gerald Lawrence—Joe started a signing group called the Keynotes. "That's what we wanted to be. We started singing after school. In the shower after gym class, we started harmonizing. You find places where you could sing. We would sing after playing basketball at Lapham Park." The group was so good, they performed in singing competitions and even opened for the well-known group the Spaniels when they performed at the Colonial Theater on North Sixteenth and Vliet Streets. "They let us sing one of their songs, and they let us use their band. That's big time when you are in the ninth grade." Joe remembers competing against great singers, such as Al Jarreau, who attended Lincoln High School in Milwaukee at the time. Jarreau went on to become a Grammy-winning jazz artist. The group stayed together until well after high school. They even sang at events throughout the city when they were in their thirties.

In his twenties, Joe got a job at Child's Restaurant on Third Street and Wisconsin Avenue. Then he started work as a parking attendant at the lot just across the street from Child's. Six years later, Joe acquired a lease for a parking lot downtown, across the street from the Pfister Hotel. He became the first Black man in the state of Wisconsin to lease a downtown parking lot. When a parking structure was built on that spot, Joe operated an underground lot a block away on Jackson and Mason Streets. He operated the lot for thirty-five years.

Joe married Sharon Coleman in the 1960s. The couple remained married for seven and a half years. He and his wife had two sons, Mark and Maurice. Maurice, the youngest, was born with cerebral palsy.

Joe was drafted into the army during the Cuban missile crisis. However, when his wife got pregnant, he was given a deferment.

RAYMOND WASHINGTON

Raymond Washington was born in Wauwatosa, Wisconsin, at the Milwaukee County Hospital in 1937. His family set down roots in Milwaukee in 1923 when his great-uncle Joe White came here from

Greenwood, Mississippi, looking for work. He found employment at Grede Foundries, a gray iron castings company in Wauwatosa. He originally resided on the East side, near Kilbourn Avenue, where many Black people settled at the time. Two years later, Joe sent for his sister Betty McMillian. She arrived in Milwaukee with her three daughters, Mattie, Raymond's mother and his aunts, Gussie and Annie. His mother and aunts were the first generation of McMillian children to grow up in Milwaukee. In the 1940s, Willie McMillian, Raymond's cousin, joined the group when he hitchhiked to from Greenwood to Milwaukee.

When Raymond was born, his family lived at 730B West Galena. They lived for a number of years in a cold-water flat at 2136B North Sixth Street. Five years later, they moved to Ninth and Walnut Streets. Raymond was the second generation of his family to grow up in the city.

Raymond Washington. *Courtesy of Sandra Jones.*

Mattie McMillian married Raymond Washington, who adopted Raymond when he was about four years old. However, the marriage did not last long. Mattie worked as a hairdresser at Gimbels Schuster's in downtown Milwaukee. She was in and out of Raymond's life. Consequently, Raymond was mainly raised by his grandmother Betty, his aunt Lula and his uncle Joe. "I was shifted around because my mother was out there. She didn't have time. But there was love wherever I went. By me being the first born here in Milwaukee, I was spoiled by them."

One significant moment in Raymond's childhood came when his mother made a home with James Clay on Tenth and Reservoir Streets. "He was the most wonderful man in my life….And so that's how I started living with my mother again, because of him," recalled Raymond. He tells the story of how displeased James became when Raymond borrowed a bike from a friend. When Raymond showed up at home, James made him take the bike back to his friend. "Take that bike back. Don't let me catch you riding anybody else's bike." The next week, he bought Raymond his own brand-new ten-speed bike.

Raymond Washington. *Courtesy of Sandra Jones.*

Raymond (*second row, second from the right*) and Bobby Mosley (*third row, third from the left*) at Ninth Street School. *Courtesy of Robert Mosley.*

Profiles

Left: Raymond with his mother and stepfather. *Courtesy of Raymond Washington.*

Right: Raymond's mother, Mattie McMillian, and stepfather, Raymond Washington. *Courtesy of Raymond Washington.*

Raymond was also very close to his unlce. His name was John McMillian, but according to Raymond, everyone called him Monkey John. Monkey John was very well known in the neighborhood. He remembers asking people if they knew Monkey John. Many would respond, "Oh that's your uncle? That was the greatest guy." One day, Raymond asked a friend of John's how he got the nickname. She told him that, growing up, John was always on the monkey bars at Lapham Park, "So, people just started calling him Monkey John."

Raymond attended Ninth Street School and St. Benedict for elementary school. He went to Roosevelt for junior high school, and he attended and graduated from North Division High School.

Raymond held many jobs over his lifetime. As a teenager, he had many odd jobs. He worked at Lloyd's Drugstore on Eighth and Walnut Streets, cleaning

Voices of Milwaukee Bronzeville

Above, left: Monkey John McMillian. *Courtesy of Raymond Washington.*

Above, right: Monkey John and his friend "Candy" Tabor standing in front of the Savoy Night Club. *Courtesy of Raymond Washington.*

Left: Raymond's children: Gayle (*sitting, front row*), Reggie (*to her right*), Kevin (*back row, left*) and Joy (*to his left*). *Courtesy of Raymond Washington.*

Opposite: Raymond and his wife, Beverly. *Courtesy of Raymond Washington.*

Profiles

up and taking out trash. He worked at the Sandbox Cleaners on Ninth and Walnut Streets, counting hangers and hanging clothes. As an adult, Raymond found employment at International Harvester, Patrick Cudahy and General Merchandise. Eventually, Raymond became a truck driver.

Raymond married Barbara Bennett in 1959. They had four children: Gayle, Reginald, Kevin and Joy.

Sharon Adams

Sharon Adams was born on January 17, 1947, at Saint Anthony Hospital in Milwaukee, Wisconsin. Her parents, Julius and Hattie Foster, and their first daughter, Joella, moved to Milwaukee from Memphis, Tennessee, in 1945. The young family left the South in pursuit of safety. At the time, Black landowners were being attacked and killed in the area, and the Fosters were among them. Their family owned two hundred acres of land in the county. While using a pocket knife to peel an apple, Julius was arrested and accused of brandishing a weapon. Hattie went to the jail and was able to get him released. Soon after, they decided to leave Memphis. Having friends who lived in the city, they decided to settle in Milwaukee.

The family initially lived with family friends Brookie and Buffus McClain. Sharon recalls her mother saying that they arrived in Milwaukee with the Mayflower. What she meant was that their furniture was brought to Milwaukee by the Mayflower Moving Company. "They came prepared to live here." Other family members migrated to Milwaukee, including Hattie's sister and husband, Bessie and Carlton Guice; her brother Harry Hutchins; and his wife, Cora. After several years, Bessie and Carlton Guice bought a duplex at 641 West Clarke Street. It was a family home for aunts, uncles and her parents.

Profiles

Opposite: Sharon's mother (*right*), Mrs. Parker (*center*) and a cousin (*left*). *Courtesy of Sharon Adams.*

Above: Sharon and her father, Julius Foster. *Courtesy of Sharon Adams.*

Young Sharon at Christmas with brand-new Rita doll. *Courtesy of Sharon Adams.*

Julius secured employment at the Milwaukee Railroad as a point man. He worked himself up to supervisor and stayed in the job until he retired. He also became a part owner of Diamond Jim's, a tavern located on Fourth Street and North Avenue. He also started Foster's Janitorial Service with the motto: "No job too big or too small." Sharon remembers, "He took me to every job that he worked. I'd go to the Milwaukee Railroad and watch my dad switch the train tracks."

Profiles

Right: Sharon holds her old friend Rita today. *Courtesy of Sandra Jones.*

Below: Julius Foster and his Milwaukee Railroad work crew. They would often join him at his home on Seventeenth Street for cards and good times. *Courtesy of Sharon Adams.*

Sharon started her elementary education at Lee Street School. She remained at Lee from kindergarten to the third grade. When the family moved to Seventeenth Street and North Avenue, she transferred to Lloyd Street School. After Sharon graduated from the eighth grade in 1960, she was enrolled at Roosevelt Junior High School. She attended and graduated from West Division High School in 1964.

At the time the Fosters moved to Seventeenth Street, the block was integrated. White families began moving away, and within a few years, the block was all Black. This was also when planning for the freeway was just beginning. Sharon recalls that her beautiful tree line street was being dismantled. Houses were starting to be demolished to make way for a planned freeway ramp. The move from Clark Street to Seventeenth Street was not only residential—it was a move from the outdoors to indoor activity. The home on Seventeenth Street became the "big house," but not for its size. It became a gathering place for Sunday dinners, holiday festivities and memorable overnights with family.

Sharon started working at the early age of eleven in the law offices of her older sister's husband. She did clerical work, filing paperwork and answering the telephone. When she was at Roosevelt, one of her teachers, Mr. Avery Goodrich, recommended Sharon for a training program run by the NAACP. She was hired as a grill and counter girl at Woolworth's on Fond du lac Avenue, the first African American hired by that company. Also on the recommendation of Mr. Goodrich, Sharon worked as a telephone operator, a Wisconsin Gas Company messenger and a teller at the Midland Bank located on Wisconsin Avenue.

After graduating from West Division in 1964, Sharon headed to college at the University of Wisconsin–Madison. Out of a student body of over twenty thousand, she was one of about ninety African American students. She remembers the Black students congregating around tables in the student union to socialize. After one year, Sharon transferred to UW–Milwaukee to finish her degree in political science. She graduated from UW–Milwaukee in 1967.

Sharon married William Johnson in 1969. When William entered a master's degree program at Wayne State University, the couple and their first child, Julie, left Milwaukee for Detroit, Michigan. While in Detroit, Sharon worked for the Girl Scouts as an organizer. Sharon's other children, William Jr. and Joanne, were born in Detroit. After ten years, she left Detroit for Rochester, New York. Still connected with the Girl Scouts, Sharon directed the Girl Scout Council for the five New York city boroughs.

Profiles

Left: The house on Seventeenth Street. The Foster house was called the "Big House," but not for its size. It was the place where family and friends gathered for holidays and other special occasions. *Courtesy of Sharon Adams.*

Below: Thanksgiving dinner at the "Big House." *Back row, left to right*: Irene and Lewis Hutchins (cousins); Bessie and Carlton Guice (aunt and uncle); Fletcher Hutchins (my grandfather) and his wife, Lillie Hutchins; John Sanders (uncle and husband of Susie Sanders); Jennie Lucas (cousin); and a family friend. *Front row, left to right*: Julius Foster (father); Sharon Adams; Joella Brady (sister); Hattie Foster (mother); and Susie Sanders (aunt). *Courtesy of Sharon Adams.*

Above: "Girlfriends." *From left to right*: Mrs. Parker, Susie, Bessie and Irene. *Courtesy of Sharon Adams.*

Left: Sharon with her three children, *(from left to right)* William Jr., Julie and baby Joanne. *Courtesy of Sharon Adams.*

Profiles

Right: Sharon and Larry Adams in the lobby of Adam's Garden Parks. *Courtesy of Sandra Jones.*

Below: Sharon and Larry Adams visiting Brownville, Tennessee. *Courtesy of Sharon Adams.*

After being away for twenty-seven years, Sharon returned to Milwaukee in 1996. "So, the reason I came back was to restore my parents' home. I found out that that was a bigger task than I imagined. This house wasn't upgraded. It still had what I learned is knobs and tools. In other words, it had that little break box not too far from the milk box." In the process of searching for someone to help with the upgrade of her childhood home, Sharon met the love of her life, Larry Adams. After only a year, the two were married. Carrying on the spirit of Bronzeville, Sharon and Larry went on to become leaders in transforming their neighborhood. The couple, along with their neighbors, founded Walnut Way Conservation Corp in 2000 and developed Adams Garden Park in 2020.

4
BUILDING COMMUNITY

The Neighborhood

There was a universal agreement among the folks I talked to that the spirit of community drew Black Milwaukee together. Neighbors mingled together and watched out for one another. Class and color differences existed in Milwaukee Bronzeville, but those differences were much less important than they would grow to be in later years. Lawyers, doctors and politicians shared the same streets with daylaborers and factory workers. Community meant, first and foremost, looking after and mentoring the children. It meant inventing ways to support families. It meant making homes out of inferior housing stock and creating space to build a cohesive society, to congregate and to recreate.

While segregation meant that the people in the Bronzeville were confined to a particular area of the city, it did not mean the community was denied essential and basic needs. Black people created their own elaborate economic and social structure. They opened and operated many restaurants and eating establishments, barbershops and beauty salons. Everything was available from dry cleaners and tailors to entertainment venues, social clubs and sports teams. The I-43 highway cut across the heart of the community, and the shops and housing stock is long gone. But that landscape still lives in the memories of some who came of age in that space.

William (Bill) Nolen, Raymond Washington, Robert (Bobby) Mosley and Joe DeCou hanging out together on Bill's deck on a Friday afternoon. The four men played together as children at Lapham Park in Bronzeville in the 1940s. *Courtesy of Sandra Jones.*

> BILL. *I go through there now, and I get a visual of what was there before. All the taverns that used to be on Juneau, you know, as far as entertainment, eating and living. Yeah, you can see where there was a restaurant, Clara's Restaurant, which was a very popular place in those days, but there's not a sign showing it, but I can visualize where it was. It's actually on the picture, but nobody would know if you weren't raised in that time, you wouldn't know that this is the restaurant where all the Black entertainers that came from out of town had to come to eat dinner.*

Many famous and well-known African Americans brought their talents to the many clubs on Walnut Street. Bronzeville residents were able to see first-class performances by big names like Duke Ellington, Billie Holiday and Louis Armstrong. However, the hotels in downtown did not cater to them, and they often stayed in the homes of Bronzeville families. Bill recalls one hotel that was open to Black guests. The Hotel Hillcrest was located at 504 West Galena Street, right in the heart of the neighborhood.

> BILL. *At that time, we had our hotel. You know, there used to be a big mansion on Fourth and Galena, the old Schlitz mansion. They made it into a hotel. If you looked at it today, it would be like one of those big mansions that you see out on Lake Drive. They tore all that down.*

Building Community

Bronzeville was a neighborhood conducive to the play of children. From each conversation with the people who grew up in the area, one gets the picture of parks and other open spaces, where children and young adults could go and feel a sense of freedom. One of the go-to fun spots was the Lapham Park Social Center. The social center had organized sports teams, a swimming pool and many other activities. There was always something at Lapham to keep the neighborhood friends occupied.

> JOE. *We always had somewhere to go. Like kids now don't have nowhere to go? We always had somewhere to go. The neighborhood we grew up in, we was all within about four or five blocks from each other. And we could go to the social center at Lapham Park. All the people in the core played up there.*

> Sharon. *I can feel the turnstile that we had to go through to get inside the park. Oh, my God. It seemed like you had entered fun times. I would also go to the swimming pool. And what was so great was seeing older guys who could really swim. They would dive, and there were a lot of talented guys that swam there.*

> BILL. *We had dances there, had a pool hall there, had a big gym. We had basketball, ping-pong.*

> BOBBY. *There were a couple of* [sports] *leagues down there.*

There was also the Riverview Roller-Skating Rink was located on Tenth Street and North Avenue, near the Milwaukee River, where a McDonald's fast-food restaurant stands today.

> JOE. *It was out of the neighborhood. We had to catch the bus to go over there. At the Riverview, they had some cats who could skate backwards. People would get on the sidelines and watch these cats back skating. Aw man, we should have had Olympics.*

The swimming pool at Lapham Park was not the only one in the neighborhood. The natatorium on North Avenue also had a pool with a library. The North Avenue Natatorium opened in 1902 at 1609 West North Avenue. Like many other establishments, it was not frequently used by African Americans until the 1950s.

The North Avenue Natatorium, with a swimming pool and a library, was opened in 1902. *Courtesy of* On Milwaukee.

> SHARON. *And we had a natatorium on Sixteenth in North Avenue, and it had a library. So, it was one of the few natatoriums that had a library and a swimming pool. And across the street, there was a drugstore where you could get ice cream. Yeah. So, here's the day in the summer. I could go and swim until I shriveled up. Then I'd get a book from the library. And then on a really great day, I could go and get an ice cream from the drugstore.*

The streetscape in the neighborhood had a very different look than it does today. Junkyards and horse barns were common, and men heading out to work on horse-drawn wagons was a typical scene back in the day. Bill and his friends would hop on the back of the wagons and ride along for a few blocks. Of course, the drivers would chase them off, but that didn't stop their fun.

> BILL. *Back in those days, we had a lot of horses, a lot of horse barns in this area. Not around here on the east side as much as on the other side of Fourth Street. But west of Fourth Street, like on Tenth Street, they had about five horse barns. On Tenth Street and Ninth Street, those were*

> *areas where they had a lot of horse barns all the way up to North Avenue. Every alley had big barns with hucksters and stuff. Every morning, you see these guys come out with their horses and come down the street, selling fruit, or else, they were junk men, and most of them were Jewish. But you know this was a more integrated area than it is now. It was mostly Jews and Blacks. They lived in the inner city along Walnut Street. We used to play up in their hay lofts and stuff up there. They come in in the evening and run us out the barn. We didn't steal anything from them. We just played up in the barn. That was one of our places that we used to hang out at. But in the evening time, they would come in and, "Get out of here. Get out."*

Stores were readily available for shopping on Walnut Street and also on Third Street. Amazingly, the locations of some of their favorite places were clear in their memories.

> **REUBEN.** *Cherry Street was just south of Somer Street. That's where the barbecue place was on Seventh and Cherry. Dr. Thomas, A white doctor who brought me into the world. Dr. Thomas's drugstore was across the street. That was north of North Avenue, near where the North Avenue Roller Skating Rink where we used to go to skate. There was a store on the southeast corner, and Kenneth's Barbecue was on the southwest corner, right across the street. And then Ruth Thomas, she had the Thomas Restaurant on Walnut Street. It was Thomas Restaurant on Walnut Street, Richard's Frozen Custard, Deacon Jones's Chicken Shack.*

And entertainment venues were plentiful; many stayed open all night. My interview subjects were too young at the time to partake in the life of the bars, but they remember their locations just the same.

> **RAYMOND.** *Everything for the Blacks was on upper Third Street as they called it. And then Twelfth Street, Twelfth and Vliet had all the stores that we wanted to go to. You had a bunch of Black-owned businesses around here. And I can vaguely remember when the taverns used to stay open all night. I can vaguely remember that. They would close for an hour so they could sweep it out or whatever they did and open right back up.*

> **BOBBY.** *Between Sixth and Seventh, on Juneau, there were fourteen taverns. There was seven taverns on one side and seven taverns on the other side. In*

just that one block. They were integrated; Whites and Blacks all went from one tavern to another. This was in the 1940s and the 1950s. My uncle had a tavern on about Sixth, between McKinley and Juneau. The taverns started at about Twelfth Street. Remember Nino's Steakhouse? The original Nino's was on Eleventh and Winnebago. And the taverns started there, and they went all the way over to Third Street.

Much of the socializing and connection to friends in the neighborhood took place outside. The kids who played together at Lapham Park rarely went to each other's houses. And porch sitting was a common, cultural occurrence. As the adults sat on the porches, the children played together on the block.

SHARON. *They're all on the same block. So, my way of being connected on the block was there was just so much porch sitting. You sat on the porch. And so, I was connected. I was younger, so it was a different type of connection. I can picture where they're just sitting on the porch. So, you know, this is before internet and all of these things. So, you sat and you talked on the porch, and I played—I played on the block with other children. And there's a family that lives next door. So, you just played— you played on the block, you played with the kids. Nothing was organized. You just ran up and down the block.*

Community Across Racial, Ethnic and Economic Lines

Community in Bronzeville extended across racial, ethnic and class lines. African American, German and Jewish families in similar social and economic situations coexisted for most of the history of Bronzeville. It was the poorest area in the city with the dilapidated housing stock, so everyone who lived there faced economic hardships. While African American unemployment was almost 30 percent in 1940, the White unemployment rate hovered around 12 percent. Consequently, strong bonds were built across differences, and the people shared their joys and sorrows.

BILL. *I would say from Juneau to North Avenue was mostly integrated. There was a White family that lived next door to me. A White family lived*

> *across the street from me, the Sebar family. You know, they were just as poor as we were—or poorer. They didn't have too much. They were all workers, you know. So, they were out hustling trying to make a living. When they started getting a little money in their pocket, they started moving out. They had the opportunity to move out where we didn't. We were still, even with money, we were still stuck in this general area.*

Income made little difference in where African Americans could live in Milwaukee. Segregation policies limited housing availability outside of the area. Bill remembers that folks in his neighborhood with the means to move to better housing and living conditions, nevertheless, remained in Bronzeville.

> BILL. *You know, like Mr. Jones who had tons of money. He didn't live no farther than Wright Street himself. Maybe he didn't want to move, though. 'Cause he had the money. He had more money than the average White person. He was the guy who ran the policy. He had the Seven/Eleven Tavern. He had all these apartment buildings. One of the apartment buildings that's left there on Fourth and Walnut now, he owned all of that. And he still lived in the same general area.*

The man Bill mentions here was Willie Jones, who, along with his wife, Fostoria, owned a great deal of property in Bronzeville, including the Hillcrest Hotel on Fourth Street and Galena and the Casablanca rooming house at 1641 North Fourth Street.

George grew up on Sixth Street, between Lloyd and Garfield Avenue, and he also recalls a mixed neighborhood, both in race and income. Many of his friends were from different economic and racial backgrounds. For him, race and economic status was not a factor in choosing playmates.

> GEORGE. *But I have to say, during a particular time, it was an integrated neighborhood. Poor people everywhere. But you grew up with the amalgamation of both rich people and poor people living in the same neighborhood. I was pals with a lot of Jews. The racial thing didn't come about until after the expressway was made.*

Mamie remembers the mixture of races in her neighborhood on North Fifth Street. But she also recalls the different economic classes. She lived among doctors and lawyers, as well as people who held political office.

> MAMIE. *We had a nice neighborhood. On Fifth Street, it was mostly White people. We had a few colored people. We lived near a person, Lawyer Hamilton, and Dorsey, LeRoy Simmons and Issacs Coggs. I did a lot of walking and signing up people to vote.*

Attorney James Dorsey, sometimes called the "Mayor of Bronzeville," made an unsuccessful run for alderman in 1936. LeRoy Simmons was the first African American member of the Wisconsin State Assembly and served from 1945 to 1952. Isaac Coggs was elected in 1952 and served six terms in the Wisconsin state legislature. He was also elected to the Milwaukee County Board in 1964. Many in his family would continue in public service to the Milwaukee community.

Living in such close quarters, people with varying backgrounds often found that they had more in common than their cultural differences suggested. Strong friendships grew across racial and class lines.

> BILL. *The Sebars had a grocery store that was directly across the street from us. Mrs. Sebar was Jewish. And my mother taught her how to knit and crochet. She would come over to our house just about every day in the afternoon. In fact, that's how* [my mother] *learned to speak Yiddish. She and Mrs. Sebar would sit at her kitchen table for hours. She would teach her friend to crochet, and her friend taught her to speak Yiddish. So, my mother used to go to the stores, and the people were Jewish, and would start to talk Yiddish. My mother was a real jokester anyway, and she used to get off on that.*

Those racial and cultural connections were also exhibited on very personal matters as well.

> GEORGE. *I remember a very significant time when my mother was talking across the fence to Mrs. Pop. Mrs. Pop was Jewish, and she was crying. And I found out later on she was crying because she was sharing with my mother what was happening over in Germany. OK,* [they were] *wiping away a whole bunch of Jews, OK.*

WORK ETHIC

The folks I interviewed each indicated that their parents and grandparents came to Milwaukee for better jobs and better lives. As employment options opened to Black people in Milwaukee industries, these folks saw their fathers and grandfathers head out to work every morning in jobs that were often hard and low-paying. And many came home to continue work in Walnut Street businesses. It was not uncommon for a person to work a traditional day job in a shop or factory and work in a business in the Bronzeville neighborhood at night.

Sometimes, drastic measures were required to feed your family. George recalls an incident after his father lost his job on a construction crew. He had been employed as a laborer for the city, working on a construction project on North Avenue and Oakland Avenue. Early one morning, he and some coworkers decided to go and get their jobs back.

> GEORGE. *I remember sitting around a wood-burning stove at six o'clock in the morning. My dad and some friends were talking about going to get their jobs back. He and his friends started out walking down North Avenue to Oakland with baseball bats and pick axes. The foreman saw them coming and told the men who were working in their place to go back to the union office. My father and his friends picked up the construction tools and went back to work. Nothing more was said of it.*

And mothers worked, too. Women were the primary keepers of boardinghouses. The 1950–51 issue of the *Negro Business Guide* listed 170 boardinghouses in the Bronzeville area. The majority of them were operated by women. Outside of the home, many women did day work.

> JOE. *My mother was a housekeeper. Mostly, all the Black women back then cleaned up rich people's houses. They cleaned up White people's houses.*

George's mother also did day work.

> GEORGE. *She did day work if you know what that is. You go and clean up other people's houses. Generally, all the day work people would meet up at some place on Third Street. Then they would be picked up and taken out to Shorewood. Mostly Shorewood, upscale White folk. And they would be picked up when they got off of work and brought back to the hood. That's the way that worked. And they would call it day work.*

Sharon got her strong work ethic from the adults around her, especially her father, Julius.

SHARON. *Well, my father worked with Milwaukee Railroad. And in working at the Milwaukee Railroad, he often came home, and his beard was still frozen. He still had ice in his beard. And we tended to him, we being Hattie, his wife, and me, because we could imagine what he had been through. He never complained about it.*

Sharon remembers going to work with her father.

SHARON. *I went with my father to every job that he had. I would go to the Milwaukee Railroad with him and watch him switch the train tracks. He would take me there, and I would be on the turntable, which is what turned the trains around. And so, I saw his work, it was just ingrained in me, that is what you did. You worked. You took care of your family. And that's what he did. He had an aspiration always to have his own work. And so, he was partnered at a tavern called Diamond Jim's, and he would work long hours there. He also had a janitorial service.*

The message for Sharon was one of responsibility. No sacrifice was too big or difficult to prevent you from taking care of your family. For Sharon, some of those memories are bittersweet.

SHARON. *I know that the work took its toll on him. My father died at sixty-six from heart failure. He worked more than one job. He didn't do it with a bitter spirit. One of the last things he said to me, and he was retired by then, it was December 19, and he called me in Detroit, and he said, "Your mother is spending all of my money." And it was just this joy about making the money and spending it on his family. So that's what work meant to me.*

And seeing their parents working so hard to provide for their families instilled that work ethic in the children. The folks that I talked with began their working lives at early ages. They grew up with the notion that if there is no way, they had to make one. They shined shoes and sold bottles and rags, they got paper routes.

JOE. *When your mother has so many kids, you know you ain't going to get no new bike. You know you ain't going to get certain kind of clothes, so you got a paper route. My mother could do nothing but put the roof over my head and [provide] some food. I got a job at a restaurant to keep money in my pocket. I used to sell rags, I used to sell paper cardboard. We sold that to try to make it. A lot of people don't know what a hustle is. We used to cash-in bottles. You could cash-in Coca-Cola bottle at two cents and get money for them.*

BILL. *We used to go on Saturday with our wagons. From the whole area, the women would come and get their groceries at the A&P. I had my regular customers. I'd take the groceries to their house, take them upstairs, you know, four or five bags, they'd give me a dollar, sometimes a dollar and a half. That was a lot of money. We started at nine in the morning, by Saturday evening, we'd have us forty dollars, forty-five dollars. That was more money than my dad had in his pocket. We hustled. And now, the men are doing the same thing with their cars.*

BOBBY. *I had a paper route, too. I had a little red wagon, and I'd scout around the neighborhood, and I'd look for scrap iron and sold it, because we had junkyards. There was a junkyard right around the corner.*

Reuben remembers shining shoes to make money when he was about eleven or twelve.

REUBEN. *And then I used to shine shoes to make money. I went up and down Walnut Street, Winnebago, in and out of taverns. It was dangerous, but I did it.*

They took that work ethic that was instilled in their young years into their teens. When the highway construction began in Milwaukee, Bill saw opportunities to make a little money.

BILL. *When they put the expressway in, just the planning of the expressway, which was gonna tear down most of the Black area, comin' down Seventh Street, we were about sixteen or seventeen then. Me and Phillip used to go in those old houses and get the window weights. These houses all had double-hung windows. We'd open up the sides, and there was a big, long weight in there. We'd get two or three garbage cans full of window weights. When they were tearing down all those houses, we were getting all the scrap metal. We would beat the junk man. When we found out a house was being torn down, we would take our wagons.*

> BOBBY. *I had an auto body place right on Walnut Street between Sixth and Seventh. And they had all these cars in this open lot right behind my house. And we were able to get scrap iron and things like that from all over the place, old fenders, and we take, and the junkyard was right across the street right on Walnut Street there, right by Obee's* [Funeral Home]. *It became Northwest.*

No type of work was out of the question for these young people—no matter how hard or how dirty. Joe remembers some of the toughest jobs he had as a young man.

> JOE. *Outside of Milwaukee, they had some farms out there. I tell some people they had farms that grew potatoes up here in the North. A lot of people don't know that today. They got places in the North that grow the same stuff they grow down south. I was in high school. Let me tell you, we got so dirty picking potatoes, when we got back home, my mother met us in the alley with a hose. She would wash us down in the basement. Then she'd let us go upstairs and get in the tub. That's how dirty we was. The potatoes had to be cut at the top, then you had to cut at the bottom. Then you put them in the basket. You take 'em up to the man and put 'em on a scale. The scale had a wire shifter. You put that basket of the scale and it weighed sixty pounds. He take that basket and put it over that shifter and shake it to get all the dirt off of it, it went from seventy pounds down to thirty-five pounds. He just point back at the field. But let me tell you how to get over. You soak a wet rag put it in the middle put that in the middle and then put that on the scale.*

LAPHAM PARK AND THE LAPHAM SOCIAL CENTER

At some point during the day, everybody came to the park.
You knew people through Lapham Park.

Life in Bronzeville was not all work. Almost every person I interviewed talked about the importance of the community gathering space—Lapham Park. The use of this land as a park dates back to 1853. Originally, a private facility called Quentin's Park occupied the site of what is now Roosevelt Middle School. Joseph Schlitz purchased the land in 1880 and created Schlitz Park (a popular beer garden). At that time, the neighborhood was home to eastern European and Russian Jewish immigrants. The city bought

Building Community

- Pre-1880: (named for the original owner of the parcel of land)
- 1880–1910: Schlitz Beer Garden
- 1910–1956: Lapham Park
- 1956–present: (named for George Washington Carver)
- 2013–present: The northern section of the park was renamed for James Beckum, the founder and tireless champion of the Beckum-Stapleton Little League.

the land from Joseph Uihlein around 1910 and renamed it Lapham Park after Increase Lapham, a well-known Wisconsin scientist who founded the National Weather Service. Around that time, Milwaukee joined other cities in the "social center movement" spreading across the United States. As a part of the social center movement, a dedicated social center was constructed in 1912. That movement's objective was to "make the schoolhouse the civic center of the community.…Here is a place where you are welcome to come and do anything that it occurs to you to do."

Mind you, the center was not built with Black people in mind. Like so many social and recreational activities in Milwaukee, segregation initially limited Black residents' access to the services at Lapham Park Social Center. However, by the late 1930s and 1940s, Black people had claimed the space as their own. The park hosted baseball and basketball league games. Social clubs were organized. Regular dances were held. The center held African American cultural events, after school and evening classes and many other activities. Lapham Park became an open-air green space, where the community came to breathe. It provided a healthy escape for kids to play and adults to learn. The folks interviewed for this book only have fond memories of their time spent at Lapham Park.

> GEORGE. *Well, Lapham Park, it was in the neighborhood. It was right… there near Ninth Street Grade School and also Roosevelt Junior High School. They had swinging bars and everything. You could run track. You could play outside basketball; you could do all those things.*
>
> BOBBY. *We went to school, then went home and maybe grabbed a snack, then headed up to Lapham Park. See, that was like a gathering place. It was a playground. They had everything there.*

Lapham Park was available after school during the school year. But the best time of all was the summer. It was accessible to kids from early morning and into the evening.

> BOBBY. *At Lapham Park, you had two sides, the girls side and the boys side, although you could go back and forth. The boys side was the most popular side, practically everybody was there. They played softball and football and everything you could think of. We had two baseball diamonds there, and at some time during the day, practically everybody was at Lapham Park. Met people through Lapham Park. You didn't even know where they lived. We never asked people where they lived. And the thing is, it was open so long, from early in the morning until about nine o'clock at night.*

The Lapham Park Pool and Bathhouse was a major attraction. Built as the result of demands for more recreational space by the Black community, the large outdoor pool was constructed at the park in 1941. Located at 911 West Brown Street and extending to Tenth and Resevoir Street, the WPA 1.6-acre project was constructed at a total cost of $250,000.[48]

> BOBBY. *The swimming pool was open in the summer time from about June to September. A lot of people don't realize how big the pool was. The pool was about a block long. Brown on the north, and it went all the way down to Reservoir. From 10:00 a.m. to 1:00 p.m., it was free. I would go home because I was only a block and a half from the pool. I would eat lunch, and then at 1:00 p.m., it would open again, from 1:00 p.m. 'til about 4:00 p.m. If it was real hot, it reopened at 9:00 p.m.*

Closing time didn't mean the fun had to stop.

> BILL. *It would close at 9:00 p.m., then we would come and jump over the fence and swim for free. We'd be in the pool 'til 12:00 at night. If you go down Brown Street and you see that little building that looks like a little office, that was the last thing left of the Lapham swimming pool.*

The Lapham Park pool was the site of the annual swim meet. This annual event generated excitement and drew huge crowds from the community.[49]

> JOE. *It was almost like the Olympic diving. Every so often, before the swim time was over, the divers would congregate around the diving board.*

Building Community

A building on Ninth and Brown Streets. The last thing left of the Lapham Park Swimming Pool. The building held showers and offices and the mechanical gear that operated the swimming pool water pumps. *Courtesy of Sandra Jones.*

> *Everybody knew and would say, "They getting together over there." They'd be trying to outdo each other. One guy would do a double flip. The next guy would try to do a triple flip.*

They all remembered champion swimmer Sylvester Sims. Sims won the Bronzeville Swimming and Diving Competition in 1944 and pulled off a major upset win in the Amateur Athletic Union State of Wisconsin high diving championship in 1945, the first Black man in Wisconsin history to win the title.[50]

> JOE. *We be sittin' at the pool and Sylvester be comin' out the locker room, and everybody be saying, "Sylvester's in the house, Sylvester's in the house." Everybody started getting in their positions so they could see. Sylvester make us wait, though. He be just walkin'. When he came out there, you could hear a pin drop. Everybody sittin there [wondering], "What he gon' do this time?" Then you remember what he did last time, and you say, "How he gon' top that? He'll come up with something." It's almost like watching Michael Jordan.*

Sylvester did not only perform great swimming spectacles; he was truly Bronzeville's Renaissance man. Sylvester came from a large family of talented athletes. His many talents included high-dive swimming, weight lifting, amateur boxing, track and semi-professional football.

> BOBBY. *See, at that time, Sylvester was grown. He was about twenty-one or twenty-two. He had a regular job. So that's how come he didn't come to the pool until about 3:00, 3:30 p.m., after he got off work. See, he grew up over there on Tenth Street and Brown. There was about twelve or thirteen in that family, and all the sons were lifeguards. And you talk about somebody built. He was like a weightlifter.*

Sims is just as well known for his prolific and masterful artwork. Bill, an artist himself, remembers Sylvester's artistic skills and that he shared his abilities with the neighborhood children.

> BILL. *He used to teach up there at that store where they sell supplies for artists. They had classes up there. He would teach the young kids up there. Instead of taking pay, he would take supplies.*

Reuben remembers the many great athletes at Lapham Park.

> REUBEN. *Some of the greatest athletes were at Lapham Park. I went to school with George Smith, and we went to elementary school together and junior high, and George could throw football all the way across Lapham Park. Nobody else could do that. He ended up working at A.O. Smith. And then another group of brothers who lived in an eight-square house on Fourth Street and Galena were fantastic baseball players. One of them could hit a ball all the way across the park. On Walnut Street, dudes would try to outrun each other or outplay basketball. And on the basketball court, we had Donald Levy, Raymond Levy and a lot of guys I grew up with. Because that's where you go to test yourself and see if you knew how to play. One guy we used to call Height because he jumped so high we just call him Height and slam the ball in the net.*

Lapham Park had many summer activities, but it also had attractions in the wintertime. One of its popular attractions was the ice-skating rink.

Building Community

SHARON. *My love for Lapham Park was really in the wintertime because they had ice-skating. And you could go there, and there was a shack where you could warm up. And if you didn't have ice-skates, you could get them. Do you know what the whip is? When you are in line with a whole lot of people, and you are going around and just holding on, and you are just making your own amusement. This guy named Stagger Lee would hold my hand, and we would zoom. I don't ever remember being cold. If you got cold, you'd just go into the shack and warm up a little bit.*

SCHOOLS

Like the housing limitations faced by the Black community, the schools available to African American children were within the confines of the Bronzeville neighborhood. For elementary education, Black children primarily attended the Forth Street, Ninth Street and Lloyd Street Schools. Roosevelt Junior High School, Lincoln High School and North Division

St. Benedict the Moor School, 1004 West State Street. *Courtesy of Sandra Jones.*

Top: Lloyd Street School, 1228 West Lloyd Street. *Courtesy of Sandra Jones.*

Bottom: Roosevelt Middle School, 800 West Walnut Street. *Courtesy of Sandra Jones.*

High School completed their academic trajectories. Most of the teachers who instructed Black children were White. In 1939, Milwaukee Public Schools only employed three Black teachers, and they primarily worked at the all-Black Fourth Street and Ninth Street Elementary School.[51] It was only in 1946 that the MPS policy of hiring Black high school teachers began to change.[52]

Building Community

William Nolen's *(first row, second from left)* first grade photograph at Ninth Street School. *Courtesy of Robert Mosley.*

Because the African American population was relatively small, school was a place where the folks in these pages crossed paths with each other. For their elementary education, Bill, Bobby, George, Reuben and Raymond all went to Ninth Street School at one point. Sharon went to Lee Street School and later transferred to Lloyd Street School. Bobby, Joe and Mamie attended St. Benedict.

While many of his friends attended Catholic schools, Bill received his education primarily in Milwaukee Public Schools.

> BILL. *At Ninth Street, I went from kindergarten to the fifth grade. When I got in the fifth grade, I went to Lee Street School. There was a drugstore on Seventh and North. I used to go to that drugstore all the time. So, we used to come there, and they used to have a soda fountain, and you could stop there and get your root beer when you came out of school. From there, I went to Roosevelt. From Roosevelt, I went to North. And from North, I went to Layton School of the Arts for two years. And then I went to work.*

Bill remarked on how things have changed since he was a student at Roosevelt Junior High School.

The students' connections with St. Benedict lasted long after they left the school. Here are former students at an alumni celebration: Mamie Thurman (*second row, second from the left*), Bobby Mosley (*fourth row, fourth from the right*). *Courtesy of Mamie Thurman.*

> BILL. *I'll tell you, you go over there by Roosevelt now. You know how you used to walk up the steps to get into the doors? They modernized the front of these schools. When you go down Walnut and look at Roosevelt now, you know they got that big sculpture there. You know that was a dead-end street. That was like a little park there—that's where the rock was. And then on the side of Roosevelt where that parking structure is, that was almost like a football field. You remember, they used to have those white birch trees from there to the school. We used to play football there because there was grass. I look at some of the teachers; all the teachers are dead that were over there.*

St. Benedict the Moor opened and operated a Catholic school for African American children in 1912. Classes were conducted for all grade levels and included a boarding school that drew students from Milwaukee and Chicago and other cities throughout the Midwest. St. Benedict was the only Catholic boarding school serving African American children in the country. Mamie described a typical day at school.

> MAMIE. *Before school, you had to go to church for a half hour or forty-five minutes. We would have breakfast, a peanut butter sandwich and a glass of grapefruit juice. For lunch, we would go to my grandmother's house for a hot lunch. Then we would go back to school. I worked with a man who taught me how to set type and things like that. We never learned anything about Black history.*

Many now-famous figures went to St. Benedict the Moor, including Harold Washington, the first African American mayor of Chicago; the comedian and actor Fred Sanford (Redd Fox); jazz musician and bandleader Lionel Hampton; and Charles Holton, who played with the Harlem Globe Trotters basketball team.

Bobby and Joe also went to St. Benedict. Bobby remembers that Black children made up most of the student body.

> BOBBY. *The whole school was at least 95 percent Black. I only had one or two Whites in my class. The Dominican Sisters out of Racine were the teachers. It was a big school. It had a playground that was at least four blocks between State Street and Highland Avenue.*

Bobby recalls that St. Benedict was known for its trophy collection because there were many excellent athletes. He also played basketball in school. He got his first job because he excelled in his studies.

> BOBBY. *I was an outstanding student. I had an A average throughout high school. I worked at Rank and Motteram Jewelry Store as a delivery boy. I used to carry watches in an old black suit bag. No one ever suspected that I had all those watches. I got the job through school. They notified the nuns that they needed someone who was trustworthy, and they recommended me.*

Because Joe's family was on welfare, school tuition for him and his siblings was supported by Fred Miller from the Miller Brewery Brewing Company. Many attribute the early success of St. Benedict to Miller's financial support.

> JOE. *They had a boarding school and a regular school. Best education. It was the best education that you could get. You never hear of a person leaving a Catholic school illiterate. They ain't going to let you go home If you can't read. You be there all night if you can't read.*

Like Bill, Sharon, who entered the schools at a later date, received her education in Milwaukee Public Schools. She attended Lloyd Street Elementary School. She went to Roosevelt Junior High School and then to West Division High School. Sharon's education began in the era of White flight from the city of Milwaukee proper. In 1950, the schools in the Bronzeville area were approximately 51.2 percent Black. By 1965, that percentage increased to 72.4 percent.[53] Many White families left the city school system for the suburbs.

> SHARON. *The composition of the students at Lloyd Street started out very White; and by the time I left, it was very Black.*

Among the things that Sharon remembers most was how much the teachers in each school cared about the students in their charge. Preparing them for the world that awaited them was a high priority.

> SHARON. *I had teachers that cared about drama and how we spoke and how we carried ourselves. Lorraine Carter was her name. She was a wonderful educator. She would have social activities. We had a program in etiquette; we had a program in public speaking. And we would have to say things, and she would correct us and encourage us. She was the teacher that groomed us.*

That strong bond continued for Sharon into high school at West Division High School.

> SHARON. *During high school, that was when the civic charge came. It was a teacher, Mrs. Perkins, who took me to the March on Washington in 1963. It was the first time I flew on an airplane. What impressed me was to see all those buses filled with Black people. And she took me to the National Council of Negro Women. To see these women having a brownstone and talking about building a monument was really something.*

However, Sharon does remember a male/female distinction during her high school years.

> SHARON. *I was one of the faster runners. But there was no track for me. And I wanted to run track. My friend Acquine Jackson, I could outrun him at the time. He had the option of being on a track team and getting a scholarship. That option was not available to me.*

Mentoring Children

Watching over and mentoring children was a huge enterprise in Milwaukee Bronzeville. You might say that taking care of the youth was a community project. Parents carried the greatest responsibility, of course; however, the responsibility extended beyond their front doors. I asked Reuben who his mentors were. His response: "Almost everybody, the whole neighborhood." He did speak especially about his grandfather who raised him, but he also spoke about others in the neighborhood.

> REUBEN. *Then we had Mrs. Karen cross the street. And so, I couldn't do anything without somebody reporting it back.*

Reuben also specifically mentioned Clarence L. Johnson, the owner and proprietor of Ideal Taylors. Johnson served as a great role model for young Reuben.

> REUBEN. *C.L. Johnson…lived across the street from us. He graduated from Tuskegee, and he founded the Booker T. Washington YMCA. And he had to go to the White folks downtown to do establish it. That's what was required. And he later went on and got his law degree.*

When he was older, Bill remembers the advice he received from his brother-in-law just before departing for the service. That advice served him well as he grew older.

> BILL. *My brother-in-law, he told me he used to give out the test for the federal government, "When you go into the army, be sure to try to do your best on these tests." By being drafted, the average person is angry when they go in there. They don't want to go in there in the first place. I didn't want to go in there. So, when I did get to those tests that he was talking about, I thought about what he said, and I tried to do as best as I could on the tests.*

Mamie and her sister mentored children as Girl Scout troop leaders.

> MAMIE. *Me and my sister led a group of little girls between the ages of ten and twelve. The troop was associated with St. Benedict. I did that for about two years.*

Two African American policemen walked the beat in the neighborhood. Felmers Chaney joined the Milwaukee Police Department in 1947 and was assigned to foot patrol in the Walnut Street area. Calvin Moody joined the force years earlier, in 1932, and many of the kids in the neighborhood looked up to them. However, Reuben remembers an incident that did not shine very brightly on one of them.

> REUBEN. *And then we had Calvin Moody, who was later a county supervisor, but Moody used to walk Walnut Street. One time, he got into a fight, and his pants were down, and word went around, "Hey Moody, we see your booty." That was all over Walnut Street.*

Truth be told, mentoring and watching over children was a community-wide project. Bobby told a story that illustrates just how watchful the entire community was over its children.

> BOBBY. *I had this old coloring book. And a kid, his name was Bobby Hunter, he wanted that coloring book. He said, "I'll give you twenty dollars for it." Next day, he came to school with twenty dollars and bought the coloring book. I told all the kids to follow me to the store cause I was going to buy everybody penny candy. Now, back in those days, twenty dollars was a lot of money. You could feed a family for a long time with that kind of money. The storekeeper took the money and gave it to my teacher. The teacher contacted the kids' parents and found out he took the money out of his mother's purse. They got the money back, and he had to give me back my coloring book.*

For George, it was his parents.

> GEORGE. *You had strong parents here, OK. They worked hard, and they weren't taking it. I remember my dad, he almost pulled a pistol on the cop one time because the cop chased me home. Said I broke a window. I don't know if I did or didn't, but I ran in the house. My dad walked out there, put the pistol in his back pocket. Now, think what might have happened. The cop said, "I want to talk to your son." My dad said, "What did he do?" Well, yeah, I'm think he broke a window. My dad said, "I'll take care of it." "But I'd like to talk to him." My dad said, "No, I think I'll take care of it." Now, suppose the cop would have advanced. You'd have a dead cop on your hands. My family, my daddy and my mother, they experienced what they didn't allow me to experience, and that was Milwaukee.*

Sharon spoke the same way about her mother and father; they were her mentors, demonstrating, by their stories and their actions, how to be in the world. Thinking of her father, Sharon remembers:

> SHARON. *He would tell stories. He'd tell stories about growing up, about jumping on and the riding the fastest horse. They had horses. And by the time he got home, his father was there. And it wasn't pleasant for him for taking that fast horse. But he told it in a way that gave a picture of the South where he was able to thrive. Now, I'm listening as a child, so it's around the fringes. He wanted to go on to school. But he told me that he quit school so his sister could go on to school. So, education was very important to him. So, it was mentoring by example.*
>
> *My father told me more than once, he said, "Sharon, you are not better than anyone; and you are kind to everyone." And so, that's how he managed that tavern. What that meant was, he cashed people's checks, they trusted him. They would get loans; he'd come home late at night with a TV* [laughter].

Sharon got the same kind of lessons from her mother. She describes her parents as yin and yang.

> SHARON. *I embroidered with my mother and baked and cooked. However, now that I think of her, she was the one that really encouraged me or supported me to go to Washington. I have her record from 1939 when she registered to vote. I don't know how she did it, you know, in Tennessee. It's how they lived.* [It wasn't so much that they told me what to do.] *It was so much of how they lived. She didn't say, "You have to give service." But when somebody was sick on a block, she would just cook up a pan of food and take it to their house. So, they complemented each other a lot in how they took care of each other, how they took care of me and how they took care of the family—and their block. So, it's really not surprising that I'm connected to the block.*

CHURCHES

Churches were among the essential institutions in the Bronzeville community. They were among the first and are the longest-lasting institutions that were founded in Milwaukee's Black community. St. Mark African Methodist Episcopal Church was the first African American church established in Milwaukee in 1869, led by Reverend Theodore Crosby. Its first home was located on Fourth and Cedar Streets. Highway construction ultimately moved the church to its current location on West Atkinson Avenue. Other churches established in the early days included Calvary Baptist Church, founded in 1895 on Seventh Street, led by Reverend J.D. Odom; St. Benedict the Moor Mission, founded in 1908 by Captain Lincoln C. Valle, located on Fourth Street; St. Matthews CME Church, founded in 1918 by Reverend W.S. Ferguson, located at 538 West Walnut Street for thirty-eight years; and the Church of God in Christ denomination, which was founded in 1919, headed by Elder Robert Anderson and held its first services in the homes of its members.

The churches were especially helpful to newcomers to the city. In addition to providing a spiritual home, they facilitated access to resources such as food, clothing and housing. The congregations in Black churches were welcoming to migrants who were coming north from deep southern states, including Mississippi, Tennessee, Georgia and Alabama. They helped new arrivals settle into new situations by creating familiar cultural surroundings.

Sharon's family were lifelong members of St. Matthews CME Church.

>   SHARON. *My life was shaped and reinforced by members of St. Matthews. It was also another lasting connection between me and my teacher Mr. [Avery] Goodrich, who was also a member. It was like 360 degrees. People were wrapped around each other at church and at school. As people moved to Milwaukee from the South, the church brought them together. And they formed clubs, the Tennessee Club or the Mississippi Club. They held teas and picnics. They formed social networks and brought their cultures right here to Milwaukee.*

Reuben's family made their spiritual home in the Church of God in Christ. He most remembers the woman who led the congregation and some of the great preachers of the day.

>   REUBEN. *Mount Calvary Holiness Church of America. Mother Evans, female, was the pastor, and her husband, Elder Evans, was a painter. That's how he made his money. But she ran the church, and he was an assistant, but she did practically all the preaching. And in the church, we had White and Black folks. I used to love to hear great preachers,*

> ministers. And they had a national Baptist convention at the arena. During that period of time, Black folks weren't allowed to stay in hotels. So, a number of ministers stayed with my grandparents because they had a big house on 807 West Somers Street, huge house. They had folks living in the basement and upstairs. And the minister was here. I asked him who's some of the greatest ministers in the country. He said you got one in Chicago, Dr. Jackson. And, of course, you had the one in New York to who was fantastic. He became a congressman. Oh, Adam Clayton Powell. That's it. So, I shined shoes to make enough to go and hear Dr. Jackson. Still remember that sermon.

In fact, Reuben can give you an almost word-for-word recitation of that sermon if you are willing to listen.

Bill's family attended St. Mark's African Methodist Episcopal Church, Milwaukee's first African American church, founded in 1869. That is the church where he was baptized. While his parents attended the church services sporadically, Bill often attended Mount Zion Baptist Church with a neighbor. "On Sundays, she would say, 'You want to go to Sunday school with me?' And I'd say, 'Okay.'" When he met Annie, Bill began attending Catholic church. After many years of attending services, he converted to Catholicism.

> BILL. *I went to church with Annie for fifteen or twenty years. She was Catholic, and the kids went. Everybody thought I was Catholic. One day, the secretary found out I had never converted. She told me about some classes and offered to sponsor me. I converted about fifteen years ago. Bobby and Joe were Catholic as kids. Raymond converted after I did.*

Bobby's family were early converts to Catholicism. His fraternal grandparents lived in tenement housing on State Street, right across from St. Benedict the Moor on Ninth Street. Because St. Benedict began its ministry in Milwaukee's African American community early, there was and remains a substantial number of Black Catholics in the city.

> BOBBY. *That's how we became Catholic. When they moved there, the school and the church were right across the street. My aunt's first job was at St. Benedict. She was the secretary there and worked for 35 years. She stayed there until she died.*

His mother's family attended St. Mark's and were avid church attenders. His mother had a beautiful voice and sang in the church choir. However, when she married his father, she also converted to Catholicism.

URBAN LEAGUE

The Milwaukee Urban League was established in 1919. Its founding mission was to assist the small and growing Milwaukee African American community to secure employment, decent housing and urgently needed social services. Located at 904 West Vine Street, it was poised in the heart of the Bronzeville community. In its early history, the Urban League was among the first places newcomers from southern states went to when they arrived in the city. The Urban League services provided something for everyone, including apprenticeship programs, job placement and business development. It focused many programs on young people. In conjunction with area businesses, the Urban League sponsored baseball, basketball and football teams, as well as boxing events. Its youth boxing program was run by nationally noted light-weight champion boxer "Baby" Joe Gans. Some of the young people who trained as boxers at the Urban League reached a level of national prominence. Young boxers trained by Gans included welterweight Jimmy Sherrer and his cousin three-time Golden Gloves champion LeRoy Allen.

Bill tells a story about receiving his own guidance from Baby Joe Gans.

> BILL. *His name was Charles Singleton. He lived right next door to me. We* [Bill and another young boy] *got into a fight, and I don't even remember what the fight was about. But we were just slugging it out, fist to fist. We must have been about seven, eight, nine years old and slugging. Baby Joe Gans come across the street. Golden Gloves was down under the Urban League. They had a gym down there. Baby Joe Gans, he grabbed me by the back of the collar, pulled us apart, grabbed the other boy. He said, "Y'all want to fight, huh?" He drug us across the street. My mom said she was watching the whole thing. He took us down in the gym, put these big old sixteen-ounce boxing gloves on us, put us in the ring. He said, "OK. Go to it!" Whoss. Whoss. The gloves were so heavy, we could hardly lift them. We fought 'til we almost fell out. Just mean. That's all it was.*

In reality, Joe Gans wasn't being mean. He was teaching a lesson. He harnessed that dispute and gave the boys a way to deal with it. According to an article in www.OnMilwaukee.com, Joe "taught every boy who came to the gym lessons in life, as well as how to put up his dukes."[54] Bill continued to box at the Urban League until he was twelve years old.

> Bill. *He was a good person, Joe Gans. And the boxing, after that, when I was about twelve, I used to go down there and box. I got in the Golden Gloves. I got knocked out. That was the end of boxing for me. I used to like boxing. But when I saw stars, cat hit me—kaboom. Uh oh. This ain't for me. I was about thirteen or fourteen. I used to train every day. Go down there every day. 'Cause I was right there, you know. And we had some good boxers. We had one guy, Donald Mason, lived over on Tenth Street; he was a national champ. Dow Rafferty, remember him? He was older than us, but he was a great boxer. This was a boxer's city. Did you know that? White and Black. We had a White boxer. He was well-known nationwide.*

Reuben also remembers the talent that emerged from the Urban League's youth boxing program.

> REUBEN. *Another guy is John Hubbard. He's a boxer. And he was so good, he was boxing in Joe Louis's boxing rinks when Joe would practice. And he knocked Louis down about eight times, and they sent him home. They said, "You can't be knocking the champion out." When he came back to Milwaukee, the cops tried to mess with him. And he had a high-pitched voice like a lady, but he was man. They tried to mess with him on the corner of third and Juneau, and he whipped up about seven or eight cops. He broke a couple of their arms. The only person that could stop him and cool him down was Felmers Chaney. Felmers Chaney saved those other policemen.*

Hubbard spent about three months in the house of corrections as a result of the incident.[55]

REGAL AND ROOSEVELT THEATERS

Originally named the Rose Theater, later renamed the Regal Theater, located on Seventh and Walnut Streets, the 425-seat theater was built in

The Regal Theater, located at 704 West Walnut Street. *Courtesy of Cinema Treasures.*

1917. Its first clientele was restricted to the majority Jewish population that resided in the area. It was only in the 1930s that the African American population gained access to the theater. The theater featured very popular cowboy shows and dramas.

> BOBBY. *We would come from the Lapham Park Social Center. We'd walk down Walnut Street and look up at the marque. If there was a movie at the top of the marque, that was the one that was going to be shown last. So, we would walk in and give the man a quarter, and he'd let us get in. If it was something you didn't want to see, you'd keep on going and go to the different cafés. When you went to the Regal, initially, in the afternoon, it was twelve cents. But Sid took that quarter, he was glad to make that extra money.*

Bill remembers that the marquee always had something to look forward to. At least two shows were usually listed:

> BILL. *They always had two shows going. Not like they do now. Sid would always put the most popular show for that last show, because he knew people wanted to see the best show. Sid would open the door. He had the*

popcorn machine right there at the door. So, he would have that burned popcorn going in that old lard. You used to get ticket bans on Sunday. Mothers, they be glad to get the kids out the house. And they'd be there all day. Sid broke that up with the ticket bans. If you saw three movies, when they were over, he could look at the ban and know your time was up.

Bobby especially remembers the westerns. He added:

BOBBY. *On some Sundays, they had three "shoot 'em ups." Bang, bang, bang.*

The Regal was not the only theater frequented by the folks in Bronzeville. People had many to choose from.

BOBBY. *We had all these neighborhood theaters. Theaters cost a quarter to get in. You could go right down King Drive, and you had about three or four neighborhood theaters right on King Drive. The Garfield on Locust Street, one on North Avenue, Century, the Franklin, the Colonial on Vliet, the Roosevelt on Fourteenth and North.*

The Roosevelt Theater was also a popular venue. Sharon and her mother, Hattie, always chose to go to the Roosevelt Theater on the corner

The Roosevelt Theater, located at 1402 West North Avenue. *Courtesy of the Wisconsin Historical Society.*

of Fourteenth Street and North Avenue. There, you could see "two hits for two bits."

> SHARON. *The neighborhood show for me was the Roosevelt. My friends Terry and Tony Taylor, they had a big family. And their father was the person that let you in to the Roosevelt. He was a big guy. I think it cost a quarter. And we could get popcorn. And on Saturdays, that would be where we would go. There would be a series of movies. And on some nights, Hattie and I would walk to the Roosevelt Theater and watch a movie.*

Black residents also had access to some of the movie theaters downtown, although they were more expensive.

> BOBBY. *On Sundays, my sisters would go to the Regal a lot. But I always like to go downtown. Downtown, they had the first-run movies. Later on, they came to the Regal Theater. When I went downtown, I had exactly the amount to go to the downtown theater. I didn't have any extra money. I walked down there because I didn't live too far. I walked right down the hill. Wisconsin Avenue, at that time, from Sixth all the way down to Riverside, was full of movies. They had movies all over the place.*

It was the newer shows in the theaters downtown that attracted Bobby.

> BOBBY. *A long time ago, there used to be a theater called the Towne. Before it was the Towne, it was called the Miller. It was between Wisconsin and Wells on Third Street. I can still remember this so well. I went down there, I wanted to see this movie. I still remember the name: Spanish Main. I go down there, and I had seventeen cents. My auntie used to give me seventeen cents. Most movies was twelve cents, and she'd give me a nickel to spend. I went downtown to the Miller then, and I'm standing outside. It cost eighteen cents to go in and, I had seventeen cents. I stood out there for a good ten or fifteen minutes, trying to get a penny.*

And when you didn't have the money to get into the movies, with a little ingenuity you could still see the shows.

> BILL. *You know what we would do? Phillip and me and Eddie, we'd all go downtown. We had money. One person would go in, he'd go upstairs in the balcony and open up the door. We'd climb up the fire escape in the alley.*

It would be four or five of us, and we'd go in. We did that just about every Sunday. I went to every show downtown, and the hardest show to get into was the Riverside.

Entertainment

The nightlife on Walnut Street is, of course, legendary. Clubs like the Metropole, the Moon Glow and the Flame were popular after-dark hangouts for people. But other, more intimate forms of entertainment were popular back in the day. Round robin card parties were big attractions for mothers and fathers after a full week of work. People would alternate hosting card parties from house to house each week.

> BILL. *They used to play cards on the weekends. That's where I get the gambling from. My mother was a gambler, too. And they used to play cards every Friday. So, they would switch houses every Friday. Well, that was something Blacks did in those days, especially older people. I didn't do it, but my mother and all her friends, and Miss Thurman, and Miss Thurman's mother. They used to have big card parties over there. That's why we all gamble. We got it from our parents. Miss Thurman goes down to Potawatomy all the time. She was down there yesterday.*

Card parties were not simply entertainment. They also provided a little income. The parties rotated each week from house to house, and each participant contributed something to a cash pot. The host would get a cut out of the pot. That money would often help with household expenses, such as contributing something toward the month's rent or buying a few groceries.

The policy game was also a source of entertainment, and it was a source of income if you were lucky enough to hit the right numbers. Some consider it the precursor to the modern-day lottery. Players of the policy game placed bets on three-number combinations (3-6-9). Numbers were selected from public sources: the last three numbers of the U.S. Treasury's end-of-day balance or of a local newspaper's published circulation number. Policy writers usually took small bets. Numbers were drawn daily. Bill described how the game worked.

The Gooden and Ard Smoke Shop, located at 1426 North Sixth Street, was the known policy headquarters in the Sixth Ward and was the alleged site of pay-offs to vice police. Gooden can be seen on the far left. *From the* Milwaukee Journal, *July 18, 1948, courtesy of the* Shepard Express.

> BILL. *This is how it worked. Every day, you had a policy number. They got the number out of the paper from the horse races. Every day, it changed. They used the last four numbers or six numbers. You could play a penny. You could play a nickel. You could play a dime. You had a chance to win some decent money—in those days, it was decent money. That's the way you bet. The same way they are betting right today. This was our stuff. Black folks had this. White folks didn't know nothing about this.*

But the policy game was illegal. Even though the activity was widespread in the community, it all happened in the shadows. Policy writers took bets with the players' names and the amount of money played written in codes in case they were detected by the law. The number drawings were held covertly and changed locations each day.

> BILL. *They used to draw numbers, and then they changed houses so the police could never know where the draw was going to be. My mother, we lived on Ninth and Vine, and there was a police box right on that corner.*

So, every time they wanted to try to raid any places, they would come to that police box. But my mother would be watching, and she'd call this number and say, "The police is looking at you." This is something I remember.

The policy games were a part of the underground economy in Bronzeville during the 1940s. The funds generated by the policy game supported the establishment of businesses, such as taverns and restaurants, that made up a significant part of the community's economy.[56]

5
LEAVING BRONZEVILLE

In the overall scheme of things, Bronzeville survived for a relatively short period of time, just forty years. The place that served as a home for so many people was bulldozed in the name of progress. Its final demise was brought on by two events—urban renewal designed to eliminate city blight and the construction of the Marquette Interchange and Interstate Highway I-43, creating a thoroughfare from the city center to the suburbs. Over eight thousand houses and local stores in the heart of Milwaukee's Black community were cleared away as a result of these events.

In 1948, Milwaukee residents voted affirmatively on an expressway bond issue. Work on the first segment of the massive thirteen-freeway system began in 1952. The initial component included acquiring the right-of-way property for the project. Objectively, that meant displacing the people who lived in the neighborhood, some for decades, from their homes. Only two routes out of the original thirteen freeway projects were ultimately completed—the East–West Highway and the North–South Highway—and they went right through the heart of the Black community.

Urban renewal policy initiatives began as early as 1948, with the passage of a national U.S. Housing Act. The intent was to address urban blight in cities across the country. Much of the housing stock in Milwaukee's inner city was constructed before the American Civil War. Thus, it was a prime focus of urban renewal efforts. The Milwaukee Housing Authority began constructing public housing in the late 1940s. Starting with the clearing of two city blocks, bounded by North Sixth, North Ninth, West Galena and West Vliet Streets, the city built the high-rise Hillside Terrace, the first public housing project designed for low-income families in Milwaukee. Between 1948 and 1956, the city cleared dilapidated housing and constructed over six hundred units, including one-bedroom apartments and five-room rowhouses. More construction followed. In 1958, the state legislature passed the Wisconsin Blight Elimination and Slum Clearance Act, and Milwaukee began its Community Renewal Program in 1961.[57]

The Hillside Neighborhood Redevelopment Program had displaced 69 individuals, 116 families and destroyed all 204 buildings located in the area between West Walnut, North Sixth, West Galena and North Elevnth Streets by the end of 1963. The Roosevelt Redevelopment Project, directly to the north, cleared all sixty buildings in the area between West Vine, Sixth, West Walnut and North Tenth Streets, and it displaced 88 families.[58]

At the same time, the Black population in Milwaukee was rapidly growing. In 1940, Black residents numbered just 8,821. Ten years later, that number grew to 21,772, and in 1960, the African American population totaled 62, 458. While segregation remained the city's norm, such rapid growth pushed the boundaries of the Black community as far north as Keefe Avenue and as far west as Twenty-First Street.

While these changes may have symbolized signs of progress toward better housing for African Americans and other low-income residents in the Bronzeville area, it came with some devasting consequences. Many families were displaced without relocation costs. Businesses that had served the community went out of existence, and along with those business went many jobs. In addition, these changes altered the sense of community cohesion that was such an important feature of the neighborhood.

Each of the interview subjects in this book have stories about finally leaving the community where they grew up. Some acquired apartments in Hillside. Others moved to nearby neighborhoods, such as Brewers Hill and Halyard Park.

Mamie Thurman is not sure why her grandmother sold her home on North Fifth Street, but in 1951, her family moved to East Garfield Avenue in Brewer's Hill, where she still lives today. The new residence was home to Mamie and Raymond, their children and her mother, Inez. Eventually, her grandmother also moved in.

After many years of marriage, Bill's parents separated, although they never divorced. That is when Bill and his mother finally left the neighborhood.

When the Hillside Projects expanded, they were able to move into the newly constructed section.

> BILL. *My mother and I moved when my parents separated. We moved into the projects. That's how I met Annie. She lived in the old section, and we moved into the new section.*

Bill's home on Tenth Street was eventually torn down to make way for the freeway. According to Bill, it was the last house left on the block before it was finally demolished. But Bill recently walked through the area where he lived on Ninth Street, and to his surprise, the tree that stood there when he was a kid remained. When Bill's sister Marion and her husband sold their home in the neighboring Brewer's Hill, Bill and Annie were able to purchase it. The neighborhood was about 80 percent White at the time. The couple raised their children in this home and still reside there today.

Like Bill, Joe's family moved into the new apartments in Hillside on Seventh and Vliet Streets when he was in the ninth grade. When he graduated high school, Joe moved out on his own.

> JOE. *When you turn eighteen, you have to leave home. When I graduated from St. Benedict, me and a buddy got a place together on Seventh and Burleigh Streets. We paid $300 a month for rent. That was $150 each. That was in 1959.*

Reuben Harpole's family home on Sommer's Street was a casualty of the freeway. They left the neighborhood when the freeway came through. According to Bobby, he never left Bronzeville.

> BOBBY. *Technically, I didn't leave the neighborhood. I never lived outside until I left for the army. I lived at 1736 North Seventh Street for twelve years, from 1939 to 1954. When my parents separated, I lived at 718 West Walnut Street, above a laundromat, for four years. When I came home from the army, I lived with my aunt Annabelle Childs at 3442 North Fourteenth Street. And I took over the house when she passed away.*

Bobby's sister Mildred Coleman stayed in the neighborhood at 2031 North Fifth Street until the last house was raized to make way for the freeway. In all, about forty-five houses in that area were ultimately torn down.

When the Fosters moved to Seventeenth Street and North Avenue in 1953, the deconstruction of Bronzeville was already underway, and it reached as far north as North Avenue. Sharon remembers how beautiful her new neighborhood was when they arrived. However, soon after, the trees that lined her block began to disappear.

> SHARON. *I remember the change. I remember going through it.* [We] *hadn't been in the house that long. I remember that we would sit on the upstairs porch. And it would just be under trees, and there would be caterpillars. And the feeling I get is a sadness in my parents. They didn't talk about it. But I remember that they had recently put in sod, which was a big deal then. Not seed, but sod. Then it was all torn up. What I know now is the amount of protection that they gave me from their pain.*

For Sharon, life went from the outdoors to the indoors. This may have been because the neighborhood was being demolished.

The movement away from the Bronzeville neighborhood impacted the lives of the people who made up that community, and it was significant in many ways. It represented the movement away from familiar surroundings, and for some, it disturbed a sense of identity.

> SHARON. *Well, I had my tenth birthday on Seventeenth Street I believe because I still was in grade school. So, I* [transferred] *to Lloyd Street. I think it jarred me. My friends that I saw every day at Lee Street, I didn't see them at Lloyd Street. And even though it was a ten-block move, it felt very different. My block on Clark Street was all Black. We didn't know to identify ourselves as Black. You didn't need to. We were all colored. And that wasn't the case when we moved to Seventeenth Street. I don't remember any incidents; it was just different.*

Just as importantly, the changes represented a disconnection from friends.

> SHARON. *Just jumping back to Lloyd Street* [School]. *I remember the principal, Mr. Bear, was all excited because so many of the houses were going to be torn down all around Lloyd Street. Pat was my dear friend, and she lived around Lloyd Street. And that whole block was torn down. It's just now getting redeveloped. Josey Heights, there are a couple houses there. But those were all my classmates. And so, by the time I left Lloyd Street School, the playground and the houses had been demolished.*

Leaving Bronzeville

New Neighborhoods

The end of Bronzeville proper did not necessarily mean the end of the spirit that nurtured the African American community there. Segregation remains a reality in the city, but changes pushed and expanded the edges of Black neighborhoods. Today, Milwaukee's population totals 587,521. Of that number, 38.3 percent are African American. They reside primarily in neighborhoods that boarder the old Bronzeville area. The people encounter new trials and new joys. As always, black people learned to make a way out of no way.

Hillside

The Hillside Terrace Projects were constructed to replace slum housing that was torn down to eliminate urban blight and provide housing for low-income families. Its original location was the two-square block from Galena to Vliet Streets and Sixth to Seventh Streets. The first installment of the projects was built in 1944, providing 232 multi-unit, multistory buildings with brick siding. In the mid-1950s, 388 units were added.

Today, the population of Hillside is approximately 80 percent African American, and two-thirds of these individuals are considered low-income. The annual household income is $25,000 or less. The projects includes a daycare center, the Hillside Boys and Girls Club, and the Hillside Terrace Family Resource Center.

The sign in front of Hillside Terrace Projects. *Courtesy of Sandra Jones.*

Halyard Park

The Halyard Park neighborhood was named for Ardie and Wilbur Halyard. The Halyards came to Milwaukee in 1923 and founded the Columbia Building and Loan Association. One of the agency's guiding principles was to provide resources for Black people "to build or purchase a home or pay off an existing mortgage on monthly payments."[59] The area is located between Interstate Highway I-43, North Avenue, Dr. Martin Luther King Jr. Drive and Walnut Street and is the northeastern tip of what was Bronzeville. The area itself was impacted by the same city policies that effected Bronzeville. Much of the housing stock was torn down to make way for the construction of the Lapham Housing Project. And about a block of the area was impacted by the construction of the freeway. Yet it was a natural area of expansion to an ever-increasing African American population and the displacement occurring in Bronzeville.

In the 1970s, a group of real estate firms organized the United Realty Group. Financed by the Colombia Building Saving and Loans, forty-three spacious, ranch-style, split-level colonial homes were constructed in an attempt to bring middle-class residents back to the area. Today, Halyard Park is a mix of low-income and middle-class families because the area includes the Lapham Housing Projects. Over 90 percent of the population is African American.

Lindsey Heights

Lindsey Heights comprises a 110-block area bordered by Locust Street to the north, Walnut Street to the south, Tenth Street to the west and Eighth Street to the east. The neighborhood was named after Bronzeville resident Bernice Lindsay, often called "the mother of the Black community." Lindsey Heights was one of the neighborhoods that was devastated by urban renewal, redlining and highway construction. Whole blocks were torn down. Rebuilding the neighborhood began in the early 2000s, when Sharon Adams and her husband, Larry, returned to the area and initiated its redevelopment. The couple founded the Walnut Way Organization, and along with neighbors, they began to clean up the neighborhood.

The revitalization of Lindsay Heights has come about slowly and quietly. Inspired by a few residents who had the courage to stand up to drug dealers

Top: The fountain in Halyard Park. *Courtesy of Sandra Jones.*

Bottom: The Lindsay Heights neighborhood sign. *Courtesy of Sandra Jones.*

and criminals and to invest their time and money in the community, people began looking at the area differently.[60]

In Lindsay Heights, 70 percent of the population is made up of low-income African American residents.

Harambee

Harambee neighborhood street signage. *Courtesy of Sandra Jones.*

Harambee is located north of the Central Business District and bound by the freeway to the west, Capital Drive to the north, Holton Street to the east and Center Street to the south. Pronounced "ha-rahm-BAY," it means "all pull together" in Swahili. By the 1950s, it had become the center of the African American community. Its population is made up of lower-middle-class and working-class families. Black people established businesses and cultural activities in the Harambee area, and in 1972, they started the annual Juneteenth Day Festival.[61] Because Harambee held the largest African American community in the 1960s and 1970s, it became the center of civil rights organizing against housing and school segregation.

NOTES

Introduction

1. Two notable books have been published that document the history of Bronzeville, with photographs that bring to life the vibrant community life of African Americans in Milwaukee during the early decades of the twentieth century: *Milwaukee's Bronzeville: 1900–1950* (Images of America, 2006), by Paul H. Geenen, with introduction by Reuben K. Harpole; and *Bronzeville: A Milwaukee Lifestyle* (2006), by Ivory Abena Black and Sally Di Frances.

African Americans in Wisconsin

2. Trotter, *Black Milwaukee*, xxviii.
3. Ibid.
4. Ibid.
5. Murphy and Murphy-Gnatz, *Stories*, 8.
6. Pengra, "Bonga."
7. Ibid.
8. Wisconsin Historical Society, "Aunt Mary Ann: Wisconsin's First Doctor: From Slave to Healer," www.wisconsinhistory.org.
9. Davidson, *Slavery in Wisconsin*, 44.
10. Trotter, *Black Milwaukee*, xxxvii.

Notes

11. Davidson, *Slavery in Wisconsin*, 33–34.
12. Ibid., 33.
13. Ibid., 34.
14. Trotter, *Black Milwaukee*, xxxvii.
15. Wisconsin Historical Society, "Black History in Wisconsin," www.wisconsinhistory.org.
16. Davidson, *Slavery in Wisconsin*, 35.
17. Vollmar, *Frontier City*, 44.
18. Ibid., 9.
19. Ibid., 5.
20. Hintz, *Forgotten Tales*, 26.
21. Vollmar, *Frontier City*, 3.
22. Milwaukee PBS, "Milwaukee."
23. Vollmar, *Frontier City*, 7–8.
24. Ibid., 6.
25. Pferdehirt, *Freedom Train*, 17.
26. Vollmar, *Frontier City*, 13.
27. Trotter, *Black Milwaukee*, 23–24.
28. Vollmar, *Frontier City*, 58.
29. Converted amount: $500 would be $15,115.75 in 2021.
30. Jones, *Selma*, 12.
31. Green, "Negroes in Milwaukee."
32. Vollmar, *Frontier City*, 47.

Creating Black Boundaries

33. Buchanan, "Black Milwaukee," 7.
34. Ibid., 7.
35. Ibid., 10.
36. Ibid., 176.
37. Gurda, *Milwaukee*, 179.
38. According to Trotter, "As late as 1940, 78.2 percent of the Afro-American population lived in the seventy-four blocks bound by W. Brown, W. Juneau, N. 3rd, and N. 12th Streets, but even within this core area…Afro-Americans made up only slightly more than half (52.8 percent) of the total population" (*Black Milwaukee*, 178).
39. Encyclopedia of Milwaukee, "Land Use and Planning," www.emke.uwm.edu.

40. Milwaukee PBS, "Milwaukee."
41. Trotter, *Black Milwaukee*, 70.
42. Dougherty, *Struggle*, 11.
43. Schmidt, "Milwaukee's Trauma Initiatives."
44. Gurda, *Milwaukee*, 359.
45. Connell, "1950s Milwaukee," 32.

Profiles

46. Trotter, *Black Milwaukee*, 45.
47. Avella, "Catholicism," 77–83.

Building Community

48. Trotter, *Black Milwaukee*, 201.
49. Geenen, *Bronzeville*, 77.
50. Ibid., 77.
51. Dougherty, *Struggle*, 27.
52. Ibid., 29.
53. Levine, "State of Black Milwaukee," 74.
54. Ehrmann, "Joe's Boys."
55. Ibid.
56. Geenen, *Bronzeville*, 8.

Leaving Bronzeville

57. Niemuth, "Urban Renewal," 11.
58. Ibid., 12–13.
59. Trotter, *Black Milwaukee*, 90.
60. Lindsay Heights, "Quality of Life Plan," www.zilberfamilyfoundation.org.
61. Encyclopedia of Milwaukee, "Harambee," www.emke.uwm.edu.

BIBLIOGRAPHY

Avella, Steven M. "African-American Catholicism in Milwaukee: St. Benedict the Moor Church and School." *Milwaukee History* 17, (Autumn–Winter 1994): 77–83. Children in Urban America Project-Marquette University, www.marquette.edu.

Black, Ivory Abena, and Sally Di Frances. *Bronzeville: A Milwaukee Lifestyle*. Washington, D.C.: Publishers Group, 2006.

Buchanan, Thomas R. "Black Milwaukee: 1890–1915." Master's thesis, University of Wisconsin–Milwaukee, January 1974.

Connell, Tula. "1950s Milwaukee: Race, Class, and a City Divided." *Labor Studies Journal* 42 (2017): 7–51.

Davidson, John Nelson. *Negro Slavery in Wisconsin and the Underground Railroad*. Milwaukee, WI: Parkman Club, 1897. www.wisconsinhistory.org.

Dougherty, Jack. *More Than One Struggle: The Evolution of Black School Reform in Milwaukee*. Chapel Hill: University of North Carolina Press, 2004.

Ehrmann, Pete. "One of Joe's Boys." OnMilwaukee.com, 2018. www.onmilwaukee.com.

Encyclopedia of Milwaukee. "Harambee." www.emke.uwm.edu.

Geenen, Paul H. *Milwaukee's Bronzeville: 1900–1950*. Charleston, SC: Arcadia Publishing, 2006.

Goodnow, Lyman. "Recollections of Lyman Goodnow." Manuscript in the Area Research Center, Gold Meir Library, University of Wisconsin–Milwaukee (Milwaukee SC 19). www.digital.library.wisc.edu.

Bibliography

Green, William T. "Negroes in Milwaukee." Undated, unidentified newspaper clipping from the Ethnic File in the Collections of the Milwaukee County Historical Society, Milwaukee, Wisconsin.

Gurda, John. *The Making of Milwaukee*. Milwaukee: Milwaukee County Historical Society, 1999.

Hintz, Martin. *Forgotten Tales of Wisconsin*. Charleston, SC: Arcadia Publishing, 2010.

Jones, Patrick D. *The Selma of the North: Civil Rights Insurgency in Milwaukee*. Cambridge, MA: Harvard University Press, 2009.

Levine, Marc V. "The State of Black Milwaukee in National Perspective: Racial Inequality in the Nation's 50 Largest Metropolitan Areas. In 65 Charts and Tables." *Center for Economic Development Publications*, 2020. 56. www.dc.uwm.edu.

Milwaukee PBS. "The Making of Milwaukee." www.milwaukeepbs.org.

Murphy, Nora, and Mary Murphy-Gnatz. *African American Stories in Minnesota*. St. Paul: Minnesota Historical Society, 2000.

Niemuth, Niles William. "Urban Renewal and the Development of Milwaukee's African American Community: 1960–1980." Master's thesis, University of Wisconsin–Milwaukee, 2014. www.dc.uwm.edu.

Pengra, L. "Stephen Bonga (1799–1884)." Blackpast, February 22, 2011. www.blackpast.org.

Pferdehirt, Julia. *Freedom Train North: Stories of the Underground Railroad in Wisconsin*. Middleton, WI: Living History Press, 1998.

Schmidt, John. "Milwaukee's Trauma Initiatives Are Meant to Heal. Now They Are at the Heart of the City's Racial Divide." *Milwaukee Journal Sentinel*, June 18, 2019. www.jsonline.com.

Trotter, Joe William. *Black Milwaukee: The Making of an Industrial Proletariat, 1915–45*. Chicago: University of Illinois Press, 1985.

Vollmar, A.B. "The Negro in a Midwest Frontier City, Milwaukee: 1835–1870." Unpublished master's thesis, University of Wisconsin–Milwaukee, 1968.

Wells, Robert. *This Is Milwaukee*. Garden City, NY: Double Day & Company Inc., 1970.

Wisconsin Historical Society. "Aunt Mary Ann: Wisconsin's First Doctor: From Slave to Healer." www.wisconsinhistory.org.

ABOUT THE AUTHOR

Dr. Sandra E. Jones was born and has lived her entire life in Milwaukee, Wisconsin. Her family migrated from Belzoni, Mississippi, and settled in Milwaukee in 1952. She grew up in the same neighborhoods as some of the subjects of this book. She was born at St. Anthony's Hospital. Jones's family lived on every block of West Wright Street, from Tenth Street to Seventeenth Street, and she attended Lloyd Street Elementary School. Her family moved from block to block, searching for better housing and more affordable rents. Depending on the size of the house, the rent ranged from $50 to $150. While she missed the experience of Bronzeville proper, Jones remembers spending Saturday afternoons watching movies at the Roosevelt Theater and going for ice cream at the Tastee Twist on Twelfth Street and Teutonia Avenue. Jones dropped out of North Division High School at the age of seventeen. She received a general education degree from Milwaukee Area Technical College, and seventeen years later, she entered the University of Wisconsin–Milwaukee as an undergraduate. She would walk across the stage at graduation after earning her doctorate degree in 2004. Jones served as the assistant director of the UWM Cultures and Communities Curriculum Development Program for six years. When she earned her PhD, she was hired at as an assistant professor in the Department of African and African Diaspora Studies (formerly the Department of Africology). She retired from UWM in 2015.

Visit us at
www.historypress.com